An Unofficial Tribute

Oprah

The Soul and Spirit of a Superstar

TRIUMPH
ENTERTAINMENT
Division of Triumph Books
601 South LaSalle Street
Chicago, Illinois 60605

Contents

Oprah Winfrey Tribute

A Lifetime of Inspiration

Oprah devotes herself to making the world a better place

By Larry Mayer

"The Oprah Winfrey Show" entered its 14th season in national syndication with continued dominance as the unprecedented leader in daytime talk shows.

Winfrey, 46, is only the third woman in history to own her own television and film production studio, joining Mary Pickford and Lucille Ball.

Defiantly and dramatically proving that the wildest of dreams can be transformed into reality with unyielding determination, faith and persistence, Oprah is the embodiment of the rags-to-almost-unfathomable-riches story. She's journeyed from being a poor, out-of-wedlock child to an international icon whose influence extends beyond the world of television into social awareness, publishing, film, philanthropy and education.

A difference-maker

Oprah's Book Club has single-handedly revived the publishing industry, and her Angel Network raised over $3.5 million in its first year to fund 150 scholarships for students in need. Her acting debut in 1985, when she played Sofia in *The Color Purple*, resulted in an Academy Award nomination.

Oprah recently launched *O: The Oprah Magazine* and announced her participation in Oxygen Media, a new women's cable network which will be integrated with various online properties.

While it seems that everything the Queen of All Media touches turns to gold, "The Oprah Winfrey Show" remains the cornerstone of her treasure chest. It's a forum she uses to provide daily doses of life-changing inspiration and spirituality to her legions of predominantly female fans, who view her more as their best girlfriend than a one-woman media empire worth more than some third-world countries.

"I think people like to watch her because she's a master of empathy," said New York City psychotherapist Sharyn Wolf, who has appeared on her show as a guest. "Other hosts will say, 'I know how you feel.' But she feels along with you." ➜

A thousand years from now when historians examine our culture, they won't find a more classic tale of living the American Dream than Oprah Winfrey. Born to an unwed mother in tiny Kosciusko, Miss., and sexually abused at the age of 9, Winfrey has defeated astronomical odds to become the richest, most powerful and most influential woman on American television.

"The Oprah Winfrey Show" entered its 14th season in national syndication with continued dominance as the unprecedented leader in daytime talk shows. The show has won every ratings sweep since its debut in 1986 and is watched by 22 million domestic viewers each week.

With an estimated worth of more than $725 million, Oprah is the wealthiest female entertainer in the world. In 1998, she was voted the most powerful person in the entertainment industry, topping such notables as Steven Spielberg, Rupert Murdoch, George Lucas and Ted Turner. *Time* magazine named her one of the 100 most influential people of the 20th century. With Harpo Productions, Inc.,

Oprah's commitment to the community never slows down. Here, she participates in a charity running event.

RALPH LAUREN
POLO SPORT

Permanent Charities
presents the 4th Annual
REVLON RUN/WALK FOR WOMEN
May 10, 1997

29157

Oprah Winfrey Tribute

Oprah Winfrey ... t officially authorized, approved or endorsed by Oprah Winfrey, Harpo Entertainment G... ... any organization

> ## "I am those women. I am every one of them. And they are me. That's why we get along so well."
>
> ### Oprah Winfrey

Winfrey inspired a Maryland woman, for one, to change her life. Crystal Phillips was a binge eater who weighed 245 pounds when she watched an Oprah show in which the host linked over-eating with inner turmoil. Motivated by Winfrey's words to embark on a trek of self-discovery and build self-esteem by writing in a journal, Phillips lost 110 pounds.

Oprah possesses a remarkable ability to connect with average women like Phillips by relating to their trials and triumphs. "I am those women," said Oprah. "I am every one of them. And they are me. That's why we get along so well."

While Phil Donahue may have pioneered the daytime talk genre, Oprah made it personal. Remember in 1988 when she dragged out a red wagon filled with 67 pounds of fat, symbolizing the weight she had lost? Oprah proved she was genuine; that she actually cared, wanted to know and, most importantly, was there to help. "I basically make a lot of money being myself," she said. "I sit and talk about what I'm interested in, so the show's evolvement has come from my personal evolvement. Doing it honestly feels like breathing to me. It's the most natural thing I do all day."

Getting personal

While constantly trying to find ways to inspire her audience and viewers, Winfrey has never hesitated to discuss her personal life. She is living proof that it is possible to not only survive disturbing and potentially debilitating events but to defeat those demons.

"I was raped at 9, and then molested from 10 to 14 by family and friends," she said. "I've been both criticized and applauded for talking about this openly. But your past is a filter that colors your life. I believe you need to address it and release it and move on."

Oprah has also openly discussed her long-time relationship with sports-marketing entrepreneur Stedman Graham; her ➜

PHOTO BY SHOOTING STAR

"The Queen of Talk" became the "Queen of Lean" when she dropped 67 pounds in 1988.

ongoing battle with trying to control her fluctuating weight, and has even admitted to experimenting with cocaine when she was in her 20s.

With Oprah, honesty is clearly the only policy — and she demands it from herself as well as from her guests and audience members.

"People of all backgrounds identify with her because she's never shied away from showing herself, warts and all," said Jeffrey Jacobs, president of Harpo Entertainment Group. "They know she's made mistakes and she will make mistakes, just like everybody else."

"She's emotionally available to people," said Victoria Secunda, a writer who has appeared on Oprah's show. "I think her great appeal is that she can be vulnerable like the rest of us."

Oprah earns about $125 million a year, but her values are the same as they were in 1975 when she was making $15,000 as a TV news anchor in Nashville, Tenn. "I still have my feet on the ground," she said. "I just wear better shoes."

Book smarts

Oprah's societal influence extends throughout every facet of American culture. Since starting Oprah's Book Club in 1996, all 33 books selected have skyrocketed to the top of best-seller lists. In recognition of her commitment to reading, Winfrey recently was presented one of the publishing industry's most prestigious awards: The National Book Foundation's 50th Anniversary Gold Medal for "influential contribution to reading and books."

For authors, having a book picked by Oprah is akin to winning the literary lottery. Jane Fitch was mired in anonymity

before her book, "White Oleander," was selected by Winfrey in May 1999. The sorrowful tale of a girl shuttled through foster homes after her mother commits murder, the story was called "liquid poetry" by Winfrey. "White Oleander" rocketed up the best-seller list and the movie rights were bought for a handsome sum.

"I was in shock," said Fitch. "I still am. I was used to having my stories published in journals with two copies of it as my payment. (Oprah's) the patron saint of American writers. Thanks to her, I get to have more of a career than I might have."

Melinda Haynes was living in a trailer with her husband Ray in Grand Bay, Ala., when her book, "Mother of Pearl," was selected by Oprah in June 1999. As a result, the book's print run ballooned from 10,000 to 720,000 copies. With royalties lining their bank account, Melinda and Ray purchased a French-style, five-bedroom home just outside Mobile. "It's like we won the lottery," said Ray, 57. "This is the house that Oprah built."

Jane Hamilton has had two books selected by Winfrey: "The Book of Ruth" in November 1996 and "A Map of the World" in December 1999.

"All these new readers gave me freedom," said Hamilton, who lives with her husband and their two children on an apple and pear orchard in Rochester, Wis. "I don't have to worry about having a real job. Oprah gave me — and my books — a bigger, wilder life than I'd ever imagined."

Heaven-sent

Oprah's Angel Network was born in 1997 as a campaign to encourage viewers to open their hearts and wallets to the less fortunate. In addition to the $3.5 million in "pocket change" and private donations that were raised ➜

continued on pg. 14

PHOTO BY SHOOTING STAR

For authors, having a book picked by Oprah is tantamount to winning the literary lottery.

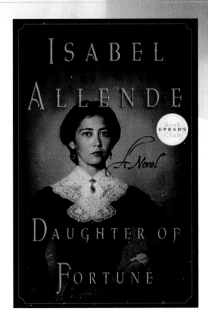

ISABEL ALLENDE

A Novel

DAUGHTER OF FORTUNE

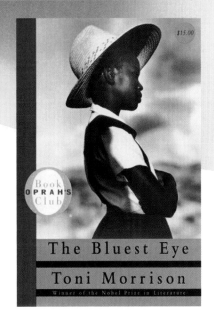

Book OPRAH'S Club

The Bluest Eye

Toni Morrison

Winner of the Nobel Prize in Literature

$15.00

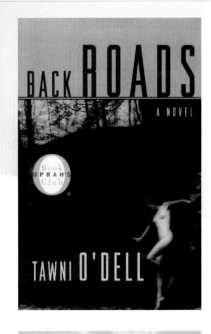

BACK ROADS

A NOVEL

Book OPRAH'S Club

TAWNI O'DELL

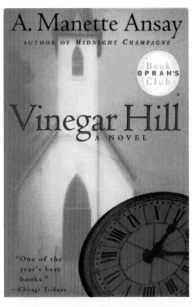

A. Manette Ansay

AUTHOR OF *MIDNIGHT CHAMPAGNE*

Book OPRAH'S Club

Vinegar Hill

A NOVEL

"One of the year's best books."
—*Chicago Tribune*

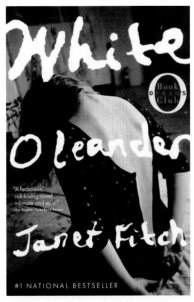

White Oleander

Book OPRAH'S Club

"A ferocious, risk-loving novel, intimate and epic."
—*Los Angeles Times Book Review*

Janet Fitch

#1 NATIONAL BESTSELLER

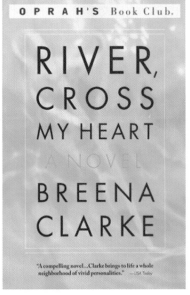

OPRAH'S Book Club.

RIVER, CROSS MY HEART

A NOVEL

BREENA CLARKE

"A compelling novel...Clarke brings to life a whole neighborhood of vivid personalities." —*USA Today*

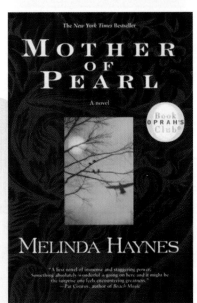

The New York Times Bestseller

MOTHER OF PEARL

A novel

Book OPRAH'S Club

MELINDA HAYNES

"A first novel of immense and staggering power. Something absolutely wonderful is going on here and it might be the surprise one feels encountering greatness."
—Pat Conroy, author of *Beach Music*

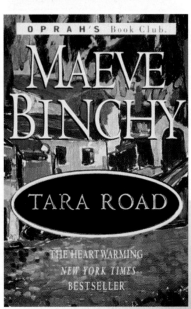

OPRAH'S Book Club.

MAEVE BINCHY

TARA ROAD

THE HEARTWARMING NEW YORK TIMES BESTSELLER

INTERNATIONAL BESTSELLER

The Reader

a novel

Book OPRAH'S Club

Bernhard Schlink

"A formally beautiful, disturbing and finally morally devastating novel. From the first page, [*The Reader*] ensnares both heart and mind."
—*Los Angeles Times*

TRANSLATED BY CAROL BROWN JANEWAY

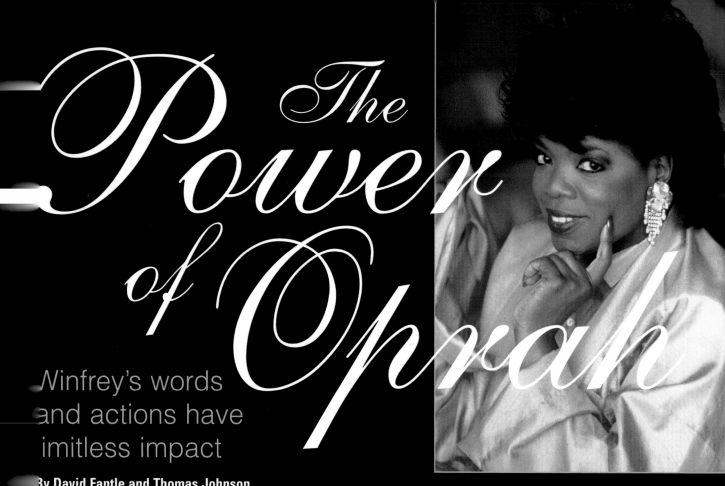

The Power of Oprah

Winfrey's words and actions have limitless impact

By David Fantle and Thomas Johnson

It may sound like a variation of an old advertising slogan for an investment firm, but in the case of Oprah, it's true: When she talks, people listen. In fact, her millions of viewers do more than just listen — they act.

As testament to the almost hypnotic power Oprah wields over her fans, when she hypes a book, it instantly becomes a best-seller; when she touts her latest miracle diet, her minions follow suit; when she unveils her latest exercise regimen, couch potatoes rise up en masse and begin sweating; when she disses the beef industry, cattle prices plummet; when she hires a personal cook and fitness trainer, those individuals achieve new levels of fortune and fame.

If there's any doubt about Oprah's widespread influence over her loyal fans, consider these case scenarios:

Book 'em, Oprah

It's no longer about winning a Pulitzer Prize or any number of other prestigious journalism awards. For thousands of aspiring authors hoping to get noticed, it's all about Oprah. Since September 1996, Oprah has selected books to discuss during a show segment she calls "Oprah's Book Club."

By plugging a particular book, Oprah has been credited with generating renewed interest in the publishing business and helping sell books — lots of them.

"I never dreamed the response would be this tremendous," said Oprah when she accepted an award from the National Book Foundation for her "influential contribution to reading and books."

In addition to promoting books, Oprah's production company recently produced a highly rated ABC movie based on Mitch Albom's best-seller "Tuesdays with Morrie."

"Books opened windows to the world for me," she said. "If I can help open them for someone else I'm happy."

Some of the books and authors that have risen to prominence thanks to Oprah include: "The Book of Ruth" and "A Map of the World" by Jane Hamilton; "She's Come Undone" and "I Know this Much is True" by Wally

Lamb; "The Deep End of the Ocean" by Jacquelyn Mitchard, and "River, Cross my Heart" by Breena Clarke.

Oprah causes a beef

It was scheduled to be just another installment of "The Oprah Winfrey Show." The topic on April 16, 1996, was dangerous foods, which included a discussion about mad cow disease. This came after the highly publicized outbreaks of the cattle disease in England.

An anti-meat guest on the show alleged that American cattle were fed ground-up livestock, a practice that some scientists suspect can spread the mad cow virus from one bovine to another. "Now doesn't that concern you a little bit right here hearing that?" Oprah asked her audience. "It just stopped me cold from eating another burger. I'm stopped."

The show caused quite a beef and led a group of wealthy Texas cattlemen to sue Winfrey for $12 million for defamation. But even before any legal papers were served, the power of Oprah was felt when beef prices plunged by $16 a head, devalued by almost 10 percent.

Winfrey told an Amarillo, Texas, jury, "If you tell me a cow has an infected brain, I don't want to eat its leg." Grilled by an attorney as to whether she believed in the first amendment, Winfrey replied, "More so now than ever before. I've been successful all of these years because I do my show with the people in mind, not for the corporations or their money."

There was no hung jury in this case. They found no defamation occurred on the part of Oprah and ruled in her favor. The beef had been settled.

Healthy living

The 5-foot-7 Winfrey made headlines in 1988 when she appeared on her show 67 pounds lighter, the result of the Optifast liquid diet plan. Soon everyone looking to shed a few pounds was following Oprah's lead. A few years later, she reached a lifetime high of 237 pounds. In between were the failed attempts at several other highly hyped diet plans.

In 1992, though, she met fitness trainer Bob Greene, who put her on a sensible diet and a rigorous exercise plan. Oprah's emphasis on fitness helped inspire millions to hit the gyms and to pay closer attention to their diets.

She also hired Rosie Daley as her personal cook. In 1994, Daley's book, "In the Kitchen with Rosie," sold 6 million copies. Greene soon followed with his own tome, "Make the Connection: Ten Steps to a Better Body — and a Better Life."

Favored with the Midas touch, everything Oprah touts turns to gold. ■

David Fantle and Thomas Johnson have interviewed more than 200 show-business personalities for publications throughout the world.

PHOTO BY SHOOTING STAR

through "The World's Largest Piggy Bank," the Angel Network also built almost 200 homes across the country through a partnership with Habitat for Humanity. Within weeks of the announcement, more than 15,000 viewers had volunteered their time and energy.

"I want you to open your hearts and see the world in a different way," said Oprah. "I promise this will change your life for the better."

Winfrey opened her heart in 1994, when she changed the focus of her show and decided to make it more meaningful.

Confrontational TV was left to the likes of Jerry Springer, Ricki Lake and Sally Jesse Raphael, while Oprah instead focused on inspiring and enhancing the lives of her viewers. At the time, she vowed "to step out in a bold way to get people to make a difference in their lives."

"I decided that I wanted to have more fun in my life, and I've been having a ball," she said. "When you make a decision, find the center of your intention, it's amazing how things just turn around.

"As a celebrity, you can make the decision to cut yourself away from the world or be part of it. I choose to be a part of it. Big time." Oprah's latest effort to soothe the soul has been the addition of a regular segment entitled "Remembering Your Spirit."

> *"I want you to open your hearts and see the world in a different way. I promise this will change your life for the better."*
>
> **Oprah Winfrey**

'Whoever saves one life saves the world entire.'

"And I want you to know that it means a lot to me, because that's really what I try to do in my life: try to reach out and save other people."

She's been at it since 1986 when "The Oprah Winfrey Show" debuted with a record-breaking launch in over 130 markets. The show currently is seen in 206 U.S. markets and is distributed to over 99 percent of the country. It's seen in 119 countries including Japan, Norway, South Africa, China, Israel and New Zealand. Every week it attracts about 25,000 letters and e-mail messages from around the world. The majority of the correspondence is from viewers commenting on the empowering, positive impact the show has had on their lives.

"I can sum her up in three words: generous in spirit," said actress Kate McGregor-Stewart (*Father of the Bride*), a guest on the show. "I was amazed at how available she is to her audience and how interested she is in being of service to them and answering their questions."

Oprah has interviewed Michael Jackson, Madonna and John F. Kennedy Jr., among others, and her show even caught a murderer in 1988 when the photograph of a fugitive was recognized by a viewer watching the show in The Netherlands.

"Oprah set the standard in daytime television," said fellow talk-show host Rosie O'Donnell. "She consistently maintains a decency and morality on her show that gives talk shows a positive name." ➜

Oprah's inner circle includes fiancé Stedman Graham, best friend Gayle King (left) and music mogul Quincy Jones.

PHOTO BY EVERETT COLLECTION

Winfrey recently showed her audience a ring she received as a gift from Spielberg, her director in *The Color Purple*. "He wrote me a note saying that he thinks that every day on the show, I try to save the entire world," she announced. "And engraved on this ring is the quote from *Schindler's List*:

continued on pg. 18

Oprah Winfrey Tribute **15**

A Lifetime of Inspiration

A Royal Connection

AP/WIDE WORLD PHOTO

Although she possessed the style and wealth associated with royalty, Diana never distanced herself from the people.

Oprah and Diana's lives intertwined by triumphs as well as troubles

By Jim Shevis

Shortly after her marriage to Prince Charles broke up, the late Princess of Wales granted Oprah Winfrey one of her rare interviews. The two had met on a number of occasions and had become friends. The interview was a mark of their affection for one another.

"I have a great deal of respect for her because she has shown that she no longer wants to be a princess on a pedestal," said Oprah of Diana. "She is the classic example of the woman who had everything, yet was not able to attain happiness."

Despite the glamour and all that a privileged life can afford, Diana struggled with her own identity: Who was she really, and what is life all about? Similarly, over the years, Oprah has sought to "find" herself as well. "I think (Diana) is a great example to women all over the world," said Oprah.

Oprah, queen of the daytime television talk shows, and Diana, the people's princess, had much in common besides their struggles to find their place in the world. Diana wielded enormous influence before her tragic death in an automobile accident on August 31, 1997. Oprah is one of the best-known individuals in American society today, reaching out to millions of viewers throughout the world. The causes they supported and the philanthropic endeavors they championed often were the same: halting the spread of AIDS; helping children; reaching out to the poor and illiterate; advancing women's causes and furthering racial equality.

In addition to her charitable work, Diana sought the abolition of land mines as weapons of war. Toward the end of her life, she visited Bosnia and spoke to the victims of mines and widows of those who had died from mine blasts. Earlier, she had done the same in Angola.

The two women shared other similarities. Just as Diana suffered from depression, which manifested itself in eating disorders, Oprah has had a lifetime obsession with food and weight, topics she has freely discussed on her television show. In "Make the Connection: 10 Steps to a Better Body — and a Better Life," a book she co-authored with personal trainer Bob Greene, Oprah recounted the anxiety she felt as the 1992 nominees for the best daytime television talk show were being introduced:

"I was 237 pounds — the fattest I'd ever been. The weight was consuming me. All I could think about was how fat I was and how glamorous all the soap stars looked."

Even though she won the award and soul mate Stedman Graham and her staff were there cheering her on, "I

> ## Oprah, queen of the daytime television talk shows, and Diana, the people's princess, had much in common besides their struggles to find their place in the world.

wanted to cry," she said. "I felt so much like a loser, like I'd lost control of my life. And the weight was symbolic of how out of control I was. I was the fattest woman in the room."

Both women took action to correct their problems. Diana went to a doctor for her bouts with bulimia and began to consult several counselors and a trainer. She attributed her eating disorder to an unsuccessful attempt to attract her husband's attention at a time when he purportedly was seeing another woman.

Oprah's weight problem was even more deep-seated. In the absence of continual parental attention, she was sexually abused as a child by a series of men. She came to grips with this victimization after lengthy counseling.

Similarities notwithstanding, the two women were different in many ways. They came from vastly different backgrounds: Diana was born to opulence as a member of one of Britain's most prominent noble families; Oprah was born and spent her earliest years on an isolated farm in Mississippi.

"I'm glad I was raised in Mississippi at a time when being colored and female meant low expectations," she said in a 1997 interview. "Now I'm grateful for my days of emptying slop jars, hauling water from the well and going to the outhouse and thinking I was going to fall in. It makes walking through the house with the many bathrooms and marble floors and a great view that much better."

Through their generosity and philanthropy, their intelligence, grace and dynamic personalities, Oprah and Diana became two of the most influential figures on the world stage. ∎

Jim Shevis is a freelance writer based in Washington, D.C.

Branching out

In *O: The Oprah Magazine*, Winfrey has developed a new medium to continue to spread her inspiration and spirituality to her fans. A review in *Time* described the 318-page debut issue as "a literary experience consistent with 'The Oprah Winfrey Show,' with the daily outpourings of emotion... Tale after tale records the triumphs of women over poverty, traumas, racism, even sexual commodification."

"You always have the potential to get better," Oprah wrote in the magazine's introduction. "That, as I see it, is one of the purposes of your life: Not to be good but continuously to get better, to constantly move forward, to create the highest, grandest vision and to be led by that vision every day."

To that end, Winfrey branched out even farther in the fall of 1999 when she joined Graham in teaching a "Dynamics in Leadership" course at Northwestern's Kellogg Graduate School of Management. Winfrey and Graham have been engaged since 1992. In expressing her love for the man she calls "Steddy," Winfrey once said, "Lots of people want to ride with you in the limo. But you want someone who'll help you catch the bus."

Oprah's closest friend is Gayle King, a former TV-news anchor who is *O*'s editor at large. Winfrey's inner circle also includes poet Maya Angelou, author Toni Morrison and music mogul Quincy Jones. Legendary for her generosity, Oprah gave King a $1 million house and is known for presenting cars, vacations and other lavish gifts to employees and friends.

Winfrey once hosted a two-day birthday celebration for Angelou at Wake Forest University in Winston-Salem, N.C. More than 200 guests flew in from Africa, England, France and various regions of the U.S. Among those in attendance were singer Gladys Knight, actress Cicely Tyson and former

AP/WIDE WORLD PHOTO

A Texas jury's rejection of a 1996 lawsuit brought against Oprah by a group of cattlemen was considered a landmark victory for free speech.

Having climbed mountains she never even knew existed won't stop the Queen of Talk from continuing to reach for the stars.

basketball star Julius Erving. "Oprah, beautiful, tough and bodacious, is the kind of daughter I would have wanted to have," said Angelou.

Realizing a dream

In 1991, Winfrey helped initiate the National Child Protection Act by testifying before the U.S. Senate Judiciary Committee to establish a national database of convicted child abusers. Oprah has established scholarships for hundreds of students and has donated millions of dollars to institutions such as Morehouse College, Spelman College and Tennessee State University, her alma mater.

She maintains such a major influence on the nation that she was sued by a group of Texas cattlemen who claimed a 1996 show focusing on mad cow disease disparaged the beef industry and caused beef prices to plummet. A jury in Amarillo, Texas, rejected the suit, prompting Oprah to exclaim, "Free speech not only lives, it rocks!"

Winfrey first learned about free speech when she began her broadcasting career at WVOL radio in Nashville while still in high school. At 19, she became the youngest person and first African-American woman to anchor the news at Nashville's WTVF-TV. She later moved to Baltimore's WJZ-TV to co-anchor the six o'clock news and eventually co-hosted a local talk show, "People Are Talking."

She moved to Chicago in 1984 to host WLS-TV's morning talk show, "A.M. Chicago." Within a year, the show expanded to an hour and was renamed "The Oprah Winfrey Show."

Even as a child, Winfrey was a skilled orator. She earned the nickname "The Preacher" and hasn't stopped talking since — much to the delight of her numerous fans. "Communicating with people is how I always developed any kind of value about myself," she said.

Winfrey's contract to do her talk show runs through 2002. She earns more than $300 million for the show's distributor, King World, which recently joined forces with CBS in a $2.5 billion merger.

Having climbed mountains she never even knew existed won't stop the Queen of Talk from continuing to reach for the stars.

"I dream about finding a new way of doing television that elevates us all," she said. "I really am tired of the crud. My goal for myself is to reach the highest level of humanity that is possible to me. Then, when I'm done, when I quit the planet, I want to be able to say, 'Boy, I did that, didn't I? Yes, I did!' And I want to get up there and high-five with the angels. High-five with them and have them say, 'Yes, girl, you did it. You really did it!' " ■

Larry Mayer is a freelance writer based in Chicago.

Angel
on earth

Oprah's generosity surpasses even her celebrity status

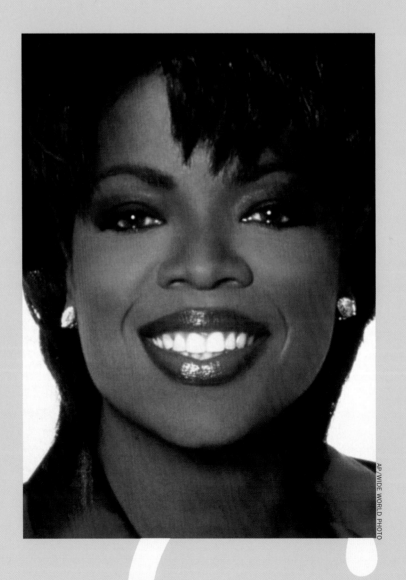

AP/WIDE WORLD PHOTO

By **David Fantle** and **Thomas Johnson**

"Think about what you have to give, not even in terms of dollars, because I believe that your life is about service. It's about what you came to give to the world, to your children, to your family."

– Oprah Winfrey, 1999

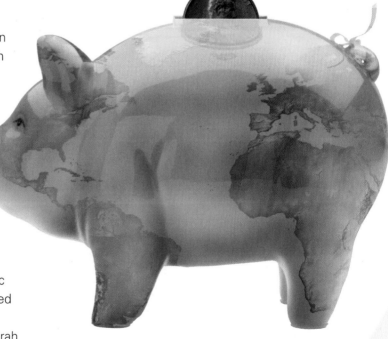

Growing up impoverished in the small rural town of Kosciusko, Miss., Oprah didn't have much to hang on to except a few dreams and an unwavering faith in her abilities. Without an abundance of adult role models, Oprah — through her vast inner strength — managed to turn her life around.

It was through hard lessons that the television host and media magnate learned to inspire people with her words and help people through her philanthropy.

Angelic pursuits

With so many requests made on her time to work on behalf of charitable organizations, Oprah decided in 1997 to funnel much of her philanthropic activities through an umbrella organization she called Oprah's Angel Network.

Announcing the initiative on Sept. 18, 1997, Oprah said, "I want you to open your hearts and see the world in a different way. I promise this will change your life for the better."

Since its inception, the Angel Network has raised millions of dollars, mostly in small contributions from Oprah's viewers. In the first year, scholarship money was raised when Oprah created "The World's Largest Piggy Bank" and asked viewers to contribute their nickels and dimes. Within six months, the bank had collected more than $3.5 million in spare change. ➜

"This is how small change makes a big difference," said Oprah. These funds helped send 150 young people to college on Angel scholarships.

Homeward bound

Habitat for Humanity is another beneficiary of the Angel Network. Based in Americus, Ga., Habitat partners with people in need to build housing that is sold at no profit through no-interest loans. To date, Habitat volunteers have built more than 60,000 houses that provide shelter for more than 300,000 people.

"This is something we can do," announced Oprah to her nearly 30 million viewers in 1997. Oprah challenged her viewers to volunteer so that a Habitat home could be built in each of the 205 markets carrying "The Oprah Winfrey Show." Viewers were asked to submit postcards, which were then distributed to Habitat affiliates throughout the country.

To kick off the Angel Network's partnership with Habitat for Humanity, Oprah presented a personal check for $55,000 to Wayne Walker, chairman of Habitat's board, to build a house for Peggy Long in Chicago, the home city of Oprah's show. Oprah and her Harpo Productions staff helped work on the house, which was completed in April 1999.

Just two years after Oprah made the on-air challenge, the goal of building 200 homes had been attained thanks to thousands of volunteers who donated their labor and hundreds of corporations who contributed the necessary funding.

Chain of command

On Oct. 19, 1998, Oprah's Angel Network entered its second year by introducing "The Kindness Chain." Oprah invited viewers to "become a link in our chain of kindness by doing something meaningful for someone who needs it. Then, if you are on the receiving end of an act of kindness, be sure to pass it on so that the chain isn't broken!"

The East Coast chain was started by "Today Show" weatherman Al Roker, who presented the Girls Choir of Harlem with new music stands and chairs. In

Oprah's Angel Network works closely with Habitat for Humanity to provide housing for people in need.

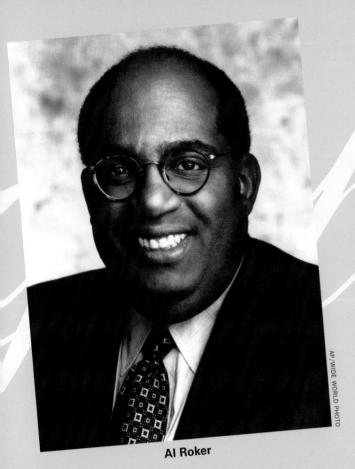

Al Roker

AP/WIDE WORLD PHOTO

Andrew Shue

AP/WIDE WORLD PHOTO

return, the Choir performed a free concert for the show's outdoor audience at Rockefeller Center. On the West Coast, actor and soccer player Andrew Shue volunteered by giving soccer tips to young players who, in turn, kept the chain unbroken by helping a neighborhood couple do some much-needed yard work.

"We want you to really begin to open up your eyes, notice people around you, and look for ways to help those in need," said Oprah.

Calling all angels

On April 20, 2000, Oprah announced another chapter in her Angel Network. Dubbed the "Use Your Life Award," this segment of Oprah's show devotes a few minutes every Monday to spotlight and fund grass-roots charitable efforts from around the world. "This is one of my proudest days in television," she declared. "It involves our Angel Network and giving away money — a lot of money!"

The objective of the Use Your Life Award is to raise awareness about individuals who are using their time to improve the lives of others. Each weekly award recipient receives $50,000 in funding to continue and expand his or her work. Information on how to get involved in the various programs is also provided. ➜

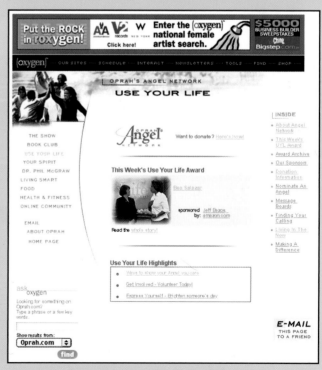

Volunteers can donate to the Angel Network by logging on to www.oprah.com.

Known for her moxie, Oprah, in addition to soliciting donations from viewers, tapped fellow multi-millionaires for funding. Acting legend Paul Newman and Amazon.com CEO Jeff Bezos are among those who agreed to pitch in.

All funds received from viewers are donated directly to the organizations recognized by Oprah's Angel Network.

"I would encourage you to look inside yourself, to see what you have to offer and use that to give back to the world," said Oprah.

More information on Oprah's Angel Network, including how to donate or nominate an "Angel," can be found on Oprah's official Web site: www.oprah.com.

Oprah's kids

Childless herself, Oprah has made the plight of children and young adults a focal point of her giving.

When she met a boy named Kalvan from the Chicago projects a few summers ago, she took him and his family under her wing and provided counseling, jobs and private schooling.

Now Kalvan and his family are out of the projects. The outgrowth of this initiative, Families for a Better Life, has received tens of thousands of dollars from Oprah in an attempt to break the chain of poverty. Her efforts continue to make a difference.

"I recognize the problem with people who are in cyclical poverty is that they haven't learned to break the chain of poverty for themselves," Oprah told

Ladies Home Journal. "You are taught to be a victim, and you can be taught not to be one."

In addition to donating money, Oprah has used her celebrity status as a stage to improve the plight of the less fortunate.

After learning of the brutal molestation/murder of a 4-year-old Chicago girl by a repeat-offense child abuser in 1991, Oprah, a child-abuse survivor herself, knew she could not just sit and watch. "I didn't know this child, never heard her laughter," said Oprah. "But I vowed that night to do something, to take a stand for the children of this country."

Oprah enlisted the aid of former Illinois Governor James Thompson to help draft federal child protection legislation that would create a national database of the names of convicted child abusers and other felons. Oprah then went to Delaware Senator Joseph Biden to help her fine-tune the bill. On November 12, 1991, she traveled to Washington, D.C., to champion the National Child Protection Act and testify before the U.S. Senate Judiciary Committee to establish the database.

Actor Paul Newman (top) and Internet mogul Jeff Bezos (left) have been major contributors to Oprah's Angel Network.

Youth improvement organization, Families for a Better Life, has enjoyed the benefits of Oprah's time and resources.

President Clinton has been a big fan of Winfrey since signing the "Oprah Bill" in 1993.

"I wept for Angelica (the young victim)," Oprah told the packed committee-room chamber. "And I wept for us, a society that apparently cares so little about its children that we would allow a man with two previous convictions for kidnapping and rape of children to go free after serving only seven years of a 15-year sentence.

"You lose your childhood when you've been abused," she continued. "My heart goes out to those children who are abused at home and have no one to turn to."

The senators were moved, and in a rare display of bipartisan politics, the bill, with a few modifications, passed both the House and Senate.

On Dec. 20, 1993, President Clinton signed what he dubbed the "Oprah Bill" into law.

Back to school

Educational institutions continue to be major beneficiaries of Oprah's giving. In addition to setting up countless scholarships, she has donated millions of dollars to such schools as Morehouse College, Spelman College and Tennessee State University, her alma mater. Oprah also serves as the national spokesperson for A Better Chance, an organization that provides students attending inner-city school districts the opportunity to attend top national schools. ➔

Generous Souls

Oprah Winfrey plays as big a role in shaping contemporary American ideals as Jane Addams did in shaping early 20th-century Chicago. So it's only fitting that Oprah is an integral contributor to the Jane Addams Hull House, a non-profit Windy City icon named for the legendary charity worker.

Founded in 1889, the South Side organization assists 200,000 Chicago-area residents through various social programs; including counseling, economic development, job placement and the combatting of child abuse and domestic violence.

This aggressive social agenda prompted Oprah to become an active supporter of Hull House, and in 1994 she arranged to give the organization the proceeds from a charity auction of her most memorable clothing outfits. The auction, which took place in California, raised $75,000 for the organization.

"I think Oprah has a need to help people, and when she feels an organization is trying to meet that need, she goes all out to help it," said Hull House President Gordon Johnson. "We were fortunate she selected Hull House at that time. Her work really helped us."

The charity auction wasn't Oprah's only contribution to Hull House. Like Addams, who dedicated her life to the community, Winfrey doesn't often stray from her mission to help the public achieve social harmony.

"Oprah has a great affinity for Jane Addams and her work," said Johnson.

"And she liked the work we were doing with individuals who were in public housing and on welfare. She's helped us with other charity work — annual dinners, funding programs. We're very fortunate to have her involvement."

Assisting a charity named for Addams seems a perfect fit for Oprah. Addams worked and lived at Hull House from its inception until her death in 1935, and in 1931 she became the first American woman to win the Nobel Peace Prize. Addams and the other workers provided services for neighborhood residents; such as a day-care center, libraries and the country's first juvenile court, to name just a few.

Despite having a full slate of professional duties, Oprah, like Addams, still finds time to improve the lives of others.

"She's very caring and very committed to helping people," said Johnson of Oprah. "And she gets great satisfaction in seeing people help themselves."

Aaron George

AP/WIDE WORLD PHOTO

Oprah doesn't mind mixing it up with fellow celebs, especially if it's for a good cause.

AP / WIDE WORLD PHOTO

The clothes off her back

Oprah has even used her highly publicized weight battle to raise money for worthy causes. In 1994, she invited 2,000 lucky winners to a clothing sale in the Grand Ballroom of the Hyatt Regency Chicago. More than 50,000 Oprah viewers sent in postcards for a chance to own a piece of their favorite personality. The benefit sale of nearly 900 dresses and other clothing accessories were put on the auction block to benefit two charities.

The event began not with a no-holds-barred shopping rush, but rather with a light breakfast followed by a silent auction of 15 special Oprah garments. Most notable among the items were a dark navy-blue Richard Tyler suit Oprah wore for a Michael Jackson interview and the purple sequined dress she wore to the 1985 movie premiere of *The Color Purple*.

The silent auction was followed by a race to the racks as frenzied fans dashed to pick up anything Oprah. Prices started as low as $10 for casual pants. One participant said shoppers grabbed armfuls of clothing and then made a beeline to the fitting rooms. The four hours of power shopping netted $75,000 for

Coretta Scott King chats with Oprah at the 2000 King Center Awards dinner.

George Dawson, 102, displays a Bible given to him by Oprah.

Chicago's Jane Addams Hull House, a community outreach organization in which Oprah's long-time steady, Stedman Graham, is involved, and Families First, a Sacramento group that provides food, shelter and education for abused children.

Wildest Dreams

A few years ago, Oprah teamed with music diva Tina Turner to help fulfill the dreams of women throughout the country. Like Oprah, Turner had overcome adversity to become a huge success in the entertainment industry. Oprah used the occasion of Turner's "Wildest Dreams Tour" and asked women to write her about their "wildest dreams." More than 77,000 women responded, but Oprah sadly admitted that most of the dreams came up short.

"To our disappointment, we found that the deeper the wound, the smaller the dreams," she said. "So many women had such small visions, such small dreams for their lives, that we had a difficult time coming up with dreams to fulfill."

After sifting through the letters, Oprah managed to grant the wishes of many. She paid off the college debt for a young woman whose mother had died; she sent a woman dying of cancer to Egypt to fulfill her wish of sitting on a camel and using a cell phone; she purchased a home for a woman who had been battered and was forced to flee her own house 17 years earlier.

Although she uses her celebrity status and her audience of millions of viewers to support a number of charitable causes, Winfrey, with a fortune estimated at $725 million, does far more than the high-profile activities she chooses to publicize.

AP/WIDE WORLD PHOTO

Oprah joins the fray during Tina Turner's 1997 concert at the Greek Theatre in Los Angeles.

Oprah will never forget the barriers she worked so hard to overcome. A few years ago, on her Gratitude Day-themed program, she put it all in perspective for her fans.

"If you focus on what you have, you'll end up having more," she said. "If you focus on what you lack, you will never have enough. That is a guarantee."

Thanks to Oprah's generosity, thousands of people in need are turning their lives around the same way a little girl from Mississippi did several decades back.

Oprah is living proof that it can be done. ∎

David Fantle and Thomas Johnson are freelance writers based in Milwaukee and Los Angeles, respectively.

- born January 29, 1954 in Kosciusko, Miss.
- is an Aquarius
- her name was supposed to be "Orpah" after a character in the bible's "Book of Ruth," but it was misspelled on her birth certificate and she assumed the name "Oprah"
- her mother, Vernita Lee, and father, Vernon Winfrey, never married
- Vernon Winfrey, a barber, was married to Oprah's stepmother, Zelma Winfrey, who died in 1996
- as a child, Oprah fabricated a break-in at her mother's home in Milwaukee, knocked herself unconscious and broke her glasses because she wanted a new pair
- attended Tennessee State University
- majored in speech and drama
- was selected Miss Black Tennessee as a college freshman
- became a radio news anchor in Tennessee at age 19
- was the first African-American anchor at WTVF-TV in Nashville
- moved to Baltimore in 1976
- began hosting the Baltimore chat show "People Are Talking" in 1978
- accepted a job to host the local morning TV program "A.M. Chicago" in 1984
- has hosted "The Oprah Winfrey Show" since 1985

- was nominated for an Oscar in 1986 for her role in *The Color Purple*
- hosted the 14th annual Daytime Emmy Awards in 1987
- produced and starred in the made-for-TV miniseries "The Women of Brewster Place" in 1989
- her $725 million fortune ranks her 359th on *Forbes* magazine's 400 richest Americans
- has won seven emmys as host of "The Oprah Winfrey Show"
- began her engagement to Stedman Graham eight years ago
- taught "Dynamics of Leadership" course in 1999 (with Stedman Graham) at Northwestern University's Kellogg Graduate School of Management
- has residences in Chicago, Indiana, Colorado and Miami
- has cocker spaniels named Solomon and Sophie
- Happiest moment: Acting in 1985 movie, *The Color Purple;* she felt surrounded by a loving family
- Trained for marathon by running at 17 minutes per mile
- Stedman Graham has posed for cover of *Racquetball Magazine*

The Oprah Show is

- Currently in 14th season of syndication
- No. 1 talk show on television and has been the third highest-ranked syndicated, first-run strip for 47 consecutive sweeps periods
- Renewed through 2000 in over 99 percent of the country, including all of the top-10 markets. Renewed through 2002 in 91 percent of the country

The *Queen* of talk

The Oprah
Winfrey Show
is a runaway
success
unrivaled by
any talk show
in history

By Lynda Twardowski

The year was 1983. A floundering talk show, WLS-TV's "A.M.
Chicago," was running out of chances to make it big. The
impetus for its creation and its lead-in, the nationally distributed
"A.M. America," went off the air nearly a decade before. Its first
host, the charming Steve Edwards, fled Chicago for Hollywood's
greener pastures just three years after that. And Edwards'
replacement, Robb Weller, also ditched the Windy City not long after
he started the job, his eyes focused on New York.

Making matters worse, the sagging show was challenged with a
life-threatening competitor when rival station, WGN-TV, picked up
the popular giant of a morning talk show, "Donahue." By 1983, ➔

"A.M. Chicago" looked better prepared to bid viewers goodbye rather than good morning.

Despite the disastrous ratings and revolving host chair, producer Debra DiMaio signed on, and with her she brought one invaluable reel: an audition tape of the show she formerly produced in Baltimore, WJZ-TV's "People Are Talking." Its co-host? One sparkling, strong and sincere woman, Oprah Winfrey.

Career move

At the request of WLS-TV station head Dennis Swanson, the then-29-year-old Oprah flew from Baltimore to Chicago during the 1983 Labor Day weekend to audition for the host spot, unsure of what was in store. Rumors of persistent racism in the city, talk of a dying talk-show format and her own personal insecurities made Oprah second guess why she had come at all. But just one walk up a Chicago street and the woman who had spent much of her life shuffling from city to city could almost hear the town itself saying, "Welcome home."

Though she later referred to Chicago as "the motherland," Oprah likely had no idea then how the city would come to embrace her. But just one month after

Oprah took over as host of "A.M. Chicago," the half-hour show rose from dead last to first place. Within 12 weeks, her local audience numbered nearly twice that of "Donahue." And by January of 1985, just one year after Oprah first aired on "A.M. Chicago," the former talk-show king, Phil Donahue, packed his bags and moved to New York City. Chicago, it seemed, only had room for one talk-show titan.

Today, Oprah is no longer just queen of the city, she is queen of the media world. Her show, now called "The Oprah Winfrey Show," is seen in 206 U.S. markets, globally distributed to 119 markets — from Algeria to Iceland to Zanzibar — and watched in 9 million households each day.

With 32 Emmys under its belt, the show has been rated the No. 1 talk show for 14 consecutive seasons. So what's the secret? Hardly a secret at all: just pure Oprah.

Described by critics as everything from robust and gutsy to empathetic and therapeutic, Oprah's straight talk and humor undoubtedly made the show a success — a fact not lost on the producers at "A.M. Chicago." In less than a year after her arrival, the show was expanded to one hour and received a new name. "The Oprah Winfrey

With 32 Emmys under its belt, the show has been rated the No. 1 talk show for 14 consecutive seasons.

The host displays one of the 32 Emmys garnered by "The Oprah Winfrey Show."

Show" was born, and the years that followed bore her indelible stamp of success.

Oprah began her reign by tossing out the typical soap-opera hunk interviews and mundane questions that shaped most daytime television talk shows and tossed audiences a curve: real people, real problems, and an honest — sometimes brutally honest — approach. Besides shows devoted to the topics of young murderers, incest and cheating husbands, Oprah occasionally turned the camera toward herself, candidly revealing her own experiences with weight loss and gain, romance troubles and even the abuse she suffered as a child. The studio audience sat enraptured, but its members weren't the only ones hanging on every word.

In Chicago to testify in a lawsuit on behalf of Michael Jackson in 1984, legendary producer Quincy Jones chanced to click over to the show (still "A.M. Chicago" then) while relaxing in his hotel room. Jones was in the process of co-producing a film based on Alice Walker's ➤

In a class by herself

While Oprah has been the reigning queen of daytime talk since her show made its debut in 1985, a few giants came before her, and even more have tried to steal her crown over the past decade and a half.

Phil Donahue was the king of talk when "The Oprah Winfrey Show" first took its original format to TV screens across the nation. But it didn't take long for Oprah to unseat the veteran host and assert her rightful position as the top daytime host in the land. Oprah's unique, natural style of opening herself, revealing her inner feelings and personally connecting with her guests, audience and viewers was a refreshing approach that Americans embraced immediately.

Countless competitors rolled along during the 80s and 90s, attempting to redefine talk television like Oprah had several years prior. Sally Jesse Raphael, Montel Williams, Ricki Lake, Jerry Springer and Maury Povich are just a few of the hosts who have tried to lure viewers by turning their stages into veritable three-ring circuses.

"I couldn't do the kinds of shows that I see some other people do, I just couldn't," said Oprah. "I've reached a level of maturity in this work myself. There was a time, when I first started out, that it was far more exploited."

Today, the talk-show arena is as crowded as ever, but

PHOTO BY GLOBE

Phil Donahue was the titan of talk until Oprah came along and started dominating daytime ratings.

no one has come close to achieving the long-term success of Oprah, whose show has been the top-rated program since the mid-80s.

"The older I get, the more centered I become and the more I think I really know about myself," she said in 1999. "What I know is that what other people do doesn't really have any effect on me. Donny and Marie, Roseanne, I don't even know who all is on this year. They'll do whatever they do. I really am just focused on 'What are we going to do tomorrow?' "

And, chances are, whatever it is will be the best thing on daytime television.

Maury Povich

Jerry Springer

Ricki Lake

On Sept. 8, 1986, "The Oprah Winfrey Show" began broadcasting on 180 stations around the nation.

A view from the stage

Alexandra Stoddard, a renowned interior designer and author of 21 books, has appeared twice as a guest on "The Oprah Winfrey Show."

"Interior design is what I do, but my books are really metaphysical," she said. "I'm a contemporary philosopher and I think that our messages are so similar. I can't tell you how much affection I have for Oprah, she does an enormous amount of good with her show."

Stoddard first appeared on the show to discuss her book, "Daring to be Yourself," and then again after she'd completed "The Art of the Possible: The Path from Perfectionism to Balance and Freedom." Both times, the author walked away having been touched by Oprah's kindness and sincerity.

"The thing about Oprah is that she's so warm and affectionate to everyone," said Stoddard. "She meets millions of people and she still manages to treat every one of them with grace.

"While I was in the Green Room before the second show, she came in and gave me a big hug and said, 'Alexandra, it's so great to see you again.' She probably does that with every single person, but she still made me feel like I was special. She's got such a fabulous warmth about her that's infectious. She lifts you up on angel's wings."

Stoddard, who travels the country for book tours and speaking engagements, has felt Oprah's impact on our society first-hand.

"I talk to thousands and thousands of people, mostly women, and I ask them who is the person they admire most. I used to hear Barbara Bush's name a lot when she was in the White House, but everybody now says it's Oprah."

famed novel, "The Color Purple." As legend has it, Jones and his partners were having trouble casting Sofia, the tough and tenacious stepdaughter of the book's main character. When Jones caught a few minutes of Oprah in action he realized she would make an ideal Sofia. He called the casting directors, the casting directors called Oprah, and though several more experienced actresses auditioned for the role, Jones and director Steven Spielberg found a winner in Winfrey.

They would not be the only ones. Through the years, Oprah has been recruited to Hollywood sound stages and sets all over the United States for film and television roles. Though the talk-show host's initial work on the silver screen pointed to a promising future — Oprah received an Academy Award nomination for her role in *The Color Purple* — it also hinted at a future filled with complications.

Big business

Time spent on her film career inevitably translated to time spent away from the show. And temporary release from her WLS-TV contract, Oprah learned after fighting for six weeks for the opportunity to film *The Color Purple*, was not something that came easily.

It became clear to Oprah that choosing guests, creating topics and developing her own format were not enough. She needed more control. To gain it, Oprah would need to move the show from WLS-TV and into syndication; she linked up with King World and did just that. On Sept. 8, 1986, "The Oprah Winfrey Show" began broadcasting on 180 stations around the nation.

Piping beyond the Chicago metropolitan area and into the living rooms of small towns across America hardly inspired Oprah to abandon gritty and edgy subjects for sweet potato pie recipes; she continued to tackle the toughest topics she could find. In one landmark show in 1987, Oprah took her crew on the road to Forsythe County, Ga., (which had been banning blacks since 1912, when a white teenage girl was allegedly raped by three black men) to tape a show on racism.

This show was taped in front of an audience composed solely of residents of Forsythe County. Of course this meant the audience contained no African Americans. Her decision provoked the wrath of black civil rights leaders and activists alike, but it was also classic Oprah. The host wanted to get to the guts of Forsythe's feelings, no holds barred. Of course, that same rule applied to Oprah. When her guests continued to refer to black ➜

Celebrity guests over the years have included the cast from the 1980s hit TV series "L.A. Law"...

...to political figures such as first lady Hillary Rodham Clinton.

people as "they," Oprah wondered aloud if the guests believed blacks came from a different planet. With a razor-sharp tongue but an open ear, Oprah created a candid conversation on race the likes of which had not been seen on daytime television.

"We came here today not to argue whether black people have the right to be here; the Civil Rights Act guaranteed them that right," she said. "Our sole purpose in coming here is to try and understand the feelings and motivations of all-white Forsythe County. That's what we do every day on this show, explore people's feelings."

By 1988, Oprah had sealed her success by tackling difficult issues, and her sensational show on satanic religions and devil worship was no different. Unfortunately, the same can't be said for a show that followed in May, one on autoerotic asphyxia — the act of cutting off the flow of oxygen to the brain while masturbating. Though the topic was certainly edgy enough to cause an uproar, it was no match for the shock that followed. The afternoon that show aired, a 38-year-old viewer was found dead, apparently of autoerotic asphyxiation. His television was left on, tuned to the station Oprah's show had aired on hours earlier. Though the man's father openly blamed "The Oprah Winfrey Show," no lawsuit was filed.

The end of that year brought better days for Oprah, however. Besides dropping 67 pounds on a liquid diet, Oprah also managed to take full control and ownership of "The Oprah Winfrey Show," with a guarantee that stations owned and operated by ABC would continue to carry it

until 1993. In celebration, she spent $10 million on a new home for the production company she owned, Harpo Productions. The money purchased and renovated a 100,000-square-foot facility on the fringes of downtown Chicago containing a television studio, three movie sound stages, a staff gym and a screening room (complete with popcorn-maker).

On a mission

In the years that followed, it became clear that Oprah was building an empire. And as the ruler of that empire, Oprah obviously recognized her responsibility to the public. The early '90s, though dotted with such sensationalist shows as October 1992's "Priestly Sins" and October 1993's "Girls Having Babies," also marked the beginning of an evolution in daytime television: the era of social consciousness. Declaring she had heard enough about people blaming their mother, enough about dysfunction, Oprah announced the time had come for her show to change. The time had come, she said, for "responsible television."

Oprah ushered in the era with a story about Angelica Mena, a 4-year-old Chicago girl who was raped, strangled, then dumped into nearby Lake Michigan by her 31-year-old neighbor. Likely the most important story of child abuse Oprah had ever broadcast, the host went much further than just airing the show. She also hired former Illinois Governor James Thompson as a lobbyist paid to draft legislation creating a national registry of known child abusers that would become accessible to landlords, employers and public officials.

Nicknamed the "Oprah Bill," the National Child Protection Bill initially was attached to the Brady Bill on handgun control. Unfortunately, when gun-control opponents prevented the Brady Bill's passage, the Oprah Bill died, too. Re-proposed on its ➜

Legendary newscaster Walker Cronkite appears on the show in 1997.

AP/WIDE WORLD PHOTO

Show of strength

"The Oprah Winfrey Show" dedicated its Dec. 8, 1999, episode to a book entitled "The Courage to Give: Inspiring Stories of People Who Triumphed Over Tragedy to Make a Difference in the World." This uplifting book includes 30 first-hand accounts from people who overcame long odds to become successful and to help others achieve their goals.

The book, written by Jackie Waldman, is intended to motivate the American public, to show that even those with debilitating mental, physical or emotional conditions can be productive members of society. Nearly all the contributors to this volume reached the conclusion that their suffering began to subside only when they devoted themselves to helping relieve the suffering of others.

"Meeting 30 new friends who endured incredible pain, yet are reaching out and helping so many others, reminds me daily of the miracles of life," said Waldman, determined not to be grounded by her own battle with multiple sclerosis.

Waldman, who made a guest appearance on the show, used non-profit Internet organization ImpactOnline to encourage viewers to become active in worthwhile causes. Thirty-six hours after the program aired, 7,500 people had volunteered to assist an organization they found through ImpactOnline's VolunteerMatch.org.

"The courage to give is the courage to put your own stuff aside and reach out and help someone else," said Waldman. "Whether or not you've had difficulties, the ability to give to others touches the best part of all of us."

In addition to Oprah, other celebrities also have stated their support to the value of "The Courage to Give" and its inspirational author. "In one of my very first speaking engagements, in Dallas, Texas, a woman named Jackie Waldman greeted me at the airport," said TV personality Joan Lunden. "And I was taken by her enthusiasm for life and for helping others."

Other memorable episodes of "The Oprah Winfrey Show" include the following:

Nov. 15, 1988 – Oprah wheeled around 67 pounds of animal fat (the amount of weight she had lost) in a small red wagon.

May 4, 1992 – In the midst of LA's post-Rodney King verdict riots, "The Oprah Winfrey Show" aired in LA's KABC-TV studios and audience members and guests — looters and victims alike — confronted each other.

Feb. 10, 1993 – Oprah interviewed Michael Jackson at his famed Neverland ranch in Southern California, unveiling for the first time the reason behind his lightening skin, a rare skin disease called vitilago.

Feb. 4, 1994 – On a show in which the topic was supposed to be juries, producers surprised their recently-turned-40-year-old boss with a surprise birthday party, attended by Aretha Franklin, Gladys Knight, Cheryl Tiegs and Phylicia Rashad.

May 1995 – Oprah hatched a six-week series of fitness and diet shows entitled "Get Movin' With Oprah" in spite of the fact that the O.J. Simpson trial was airing. Her words? "...It's O.J. month anyway, and you can't fight O.J. So what do we have to do but lose a couple thousand pounds across the country?"

April 16, 1996 – An anti-meat activist alleged on the show that American cattle are fed ground-up livestock, a practice that caused the deadly mad cow disease in England. Oprah wrote off hamburgers for good. "It just stopped me from eating another burger. I'm stopped." The next day, beef prices fell sharply.

Jan. 26, 1998 – Since she had to temporarily relocate to Texas for "the great beef trial," Oprah began a series of air dates from Amarillo called "An Introduction to Texas." The four-week slate of shows was called "A Salute to Texas."

Rosie O'Donnell and Oprah shared the 1998 Daytime Emmy Award for Best Talk Show Host.

O'Donnell makes a guest appearance on "The Oprah Winfrey Show," May 19, 1997.

own, the Oprah Bill eventually passed Congress and was signed into law in 1993 by President Bill Clinton. It was a rousing victory for Oprah; so too was being recognized as the wealthiest entertainer in America by *Forbes* magazine in September 1993.

Nevertheless, with her syndication contract with King World expiring in 1995, Oprah was none to eager to re-sign. While she had remained true to her 1994 promise to refocus the show on uplifting and meaningful topics, rumors abounded that she was upset by King World's recently launched talk show, "Rolanda," which was strikingly similar to her own show. No doubt constant tabloid reports on the fluctuations of Oprah's weight and her relationship with long-time companion Stedman Graham didn't help matters.

Despite it all Oprah's ratings continued to soar and by March 21 the savvy businesswoman had signed on until the year 2000, provided King World added 1.5 million shares of King World stock to the 1 million she already owned. With both sides pleased with the contract, Oprah pushed on with sweeping changes.

In 1996, she kick-started a literary revolution with Oprah's Book Club. The on-air reading club features authors and selected guests at dinner with Oprah discussing a book of her choosing. Oprah's Book Club generally features an uplifting and powerful novel dealing with the lives of women and blacks, and written by novelists like Maya Angelou and Toni Morrison. To her credit, every book Oprah has selected has immediately become a best-seller.

Following on the book club's heels, Oprah launched her Angel Network in 1997, a campaign to encourage people to help others. The Angel Network sponsors projects like "The World's Largest Piggy Bank," a program that collects small change and uses it to fund scholarships for 50 students every year, and helping to fund Habitat for Humanity homes built for low-income families in every one of the markets in which "The Oprah Winfrey Show" airs. True to her word, Oprah's Angel Network raised more than $3.5 million in spare change and donations.

A new look

By September of 1998, the stage was set for "Change Your Life TV," Oprah's vision of what television ought to be — stimulating, thought-provoking, and a vehicle for the greater good. The *Chicago Sun-Times* nicknamed the star "Deepak-Oprah," and critics guffawed at the new-age, "touchy-feely" format.

Critics assembled even more quickly when one of the first shows of the new format featured Oprah and "Men Are From Mars, Women Are From Venus" author John Gray inviting an audience member to eliminate her I-can-never-do-enough feelings by beating a large red box labeled "Guilt" with a stick. And while some viewers tuned out, most seemed to take to the change.

Oprah, now the voice behind her show's theme song, became the voice of every woman, urging each to remember their spirit, find their passion and "run on." Millions of women heeded the call.

Miami viewer Carla Hill is one of the millions inspired by Oprah. "I've been thinking about acting for a long time now," she said. "I was very involved in high school and college. I recently had a kidney transplant and decided to stop wasting time. The show that really sparked me was the recent one on women who work, doing what they loved. They were all so... satisfied."

Of course, sparking dreams may be Oprah's forte, but with millions of viewers, Oprah also has been responsible for sparking some trouble. The 1996 show, "Dangerous Foods," featured guest Howard Lyman raising the prospect that Britain's mad cow disease scare could just as easily break out in the United States and "...make AIDS look like the common cold."

The next day, beef prices reportedly plunged, and in 1998, Amarillo cattlemen took the star to court over the eventual 10-percent devaluation of their product. Though she later admitted the weeks of stress and worry caused her great pain, Oprah appeared to have taken the suit in stride. She moved her personal entourage into Amarillo's Adaberrylinn Hotel and her show into the city's Little Theatre, where she continued to tape five shows each week, in addition to testifying in court. At the end of February, the judge declared Oprah was not liable for any damages.

It's no question that "The Oprah Winfrey Show" has created a place for itself in the history of American culture. And perhaps the best news for Oprah fans has been her decision to continue to produce and host the show through 2002 — challenging herself to come up with new, ground-breaking topics every day. And to think, that celebrated stroll down her first Chicago street seems like just yesterday. ■

Lynda Twardowski is a freelance writer based in Los Angeles.

O: The Oprah Magazine

Letter Perfect

By Sam Goldman

makes a grand debut

PHOTO BY RETNA

Oprah set out to produce a magazine that would provide inspiration for women, and, with her unique stamp all over the publication, she has undoubtedly succeeded.

Oprah's most recent triumph was an unexpected one. Though she has appeared on the covers of scores of publications, this year she launched her own magazine.

Oprah said she saw a lack of publications out there that gave women what she felt they deserved: inspiration. And that's exactly what *O: The Oprah Magazine* provides.

O has been called "the *Martha Stewart Living* for the soul." The magazine made its debut in April with a 318-page issue — every one of them 100-percent Winfrey.

"The magazine is the book that I never wrote," Oprah said. "It's an opportunity every month to use my voice, but also to share what I have learned."

The publication is packed with heartfelt stories about women who have triumphed over terrible circumstances, from poverty to racism.

Articles portray tales of women starting over and conquering adversity. The biggest feature in the first issue is a Q&A session with Oprah and Camille Cosby, wife of well-known entertainer Bill Cosby. The interview, during which Camille speaks candidly about the 1997 murder of her son, Ennis Cosby, is the first Oprah has ever done without television cameras.

Oprah's unique stamp is all over the magazine. Besides being on the cover (and she'll be on the cover for the foreseeable future), she writes two columns in every issue. "Let's Talk" opens the magazine, and the other, "What I Know For Sure," closes it. There's a calendar featuring entries like, "Ask yourself what you're really afraid of."

Frequent guests on Oprah's daytime talk show pop up in the magazine. There are advice columns from financial guru Suze Orman, fitness expert Bob Greene,

relationship consultant Philip McGraw and personal-growth writer Gary Zukav. There's even a feature on the book that changed Oprah's life.

Among Oprah's personal favorite pieces in the first issue are Marianne Williamson's thoughts on wisdom and courage and a tranquil, two-page photo of a chair at the edge of a lake. There will be one of these scenes in every issue.

When the magazine does write about typical women's magazine topics — such as food, health and fitness — it isn't condescending. One example is the piece, "Five Fabulous Things to Do with Fresh Strawberries," which ends with a quote from novelist Toni Morrison.

There are stories about hair maintenance, but no mention of specific products. There will never be a story, Oprah said, about how to get thin thighs. After all, this is Oprah, and she wants to empower women.

While the models in the first issue are racially diverse, the women featured in the second issue will also be of varying weights — up to sizes 12 and 14, the most common women's sizes. Even the ads in the magazine have been Oprah-approved: there are neither cigarette spots nor diet ads.

It wouldn't be Oprah unless she also included ways for readers to help themselves. She has called her magazine "a personal-growth guide."

O comes with lots of semi-blank pages and encourages journaling. It asks readers to write things down that they'd like to change about themselves. Typical of the questions the magazine asks the reader is "What is my heart's deepest desire?"

As Oprah writes in the first issue, "You always have the potential to get better... that, as I see it, is one of the purposes of your life. Not to be good but continuously to get better, to constantly move forward, to create the highest, grandest vision and to be led by that vision every day."

There are also postcards filled with inspirational sayings — called "Oprah to Go" — that readers can pull out and tape to their refrigerators. There's a section called "My Journal," where notable newsmakers (in the first issue, singer Jewel) share intimate thoughts.

PHOTO BY RETNA

O has been called "the *Martha Stewart Living* for the soul," and it's likely to provide some friendly competition between the long-time acquaintances.

Even while putting together her daily show, Oprah was intimately involved with the first issue of the magazine. She tried every fashion item in the "O List," which is a list of things Oprah loves, such as cozy pajamas, distinctive candles, shoes and a bag of potato chips. Oprah's best friend, Gayle King, is the magazine's Editor at Large and represents Oprah at the editorial meetings in Manhattan. From Chicago, the perfectionist Oprah reads every story, asking for rewrites up until the very last minute.

She even insists that the table of contents, usually found around page 20 of most women's magazines, be placed on page 2 so the magazine doesn't look too ad-heavy. She also demanded a change in the words on the premiere issue's cover. "Originally, they had 'Reach Any Goal in Five Simple Steps,' and I said that's exactly what I said in the first meeting that I didn't want," Oprah said. "There is not a goal in life you can reach in five steps."

Sales have been spectacular. The magazine premiered with a May/June issue and was a virtual sell-out in many cities. The original print run of 1.1 million copies wasn't large enough to meet the demand, so publishers printed another 500,000 magazines.

O will become a monthly beginning with the September issue. Can *Oprah Weekly* be far behind? ■

Sam Goldman is a freelance writer based in New York City.

PHOTO BY RETNA

An A for O

PHOTOS BY SHOOTING STAR (3)   PHOTO BY RETNA

Laurel Smoke

Dr. Samir Husni, known in publishing circles as "Mr. Magazine" for his industry expertise, recently offered his opinion on Oprah's latest endeavor, *O: The Oprah Magazine*.

"The woman has proved that anything she touches becomes hot," said Husni, a journalism professor at the University of Mississippi. "Oprah is one of the few instances in which a TV personality becomes a brand. She has taken her star power and used it to launch the magazine."

Though many experts predicted that Oprah's popularity and appearance on the cover would translate into brisk sales of the premiere issue, few expected the magazines to literally disappear overnight.

"I can't think of any other magazine that sold out more than 1 million copies in six hours," said Husni. "If someone is an Oprah fan, they will buy anything with her on it. After the magazine has been established, and she is no longer on the cover, the 'O' alone will make you think of Oprah."

But the future success of *O* will depend on more than the curiosity and hype that surrounded the premiere issue. And the magazine is up to the test, according to Husni.

"You can always sell a first issue based on the cover, but you need content to bring them back. *O* magazine has the content to bring people back."

"The magazine reflects a mission in life," he added. "Oprah has been preaching her gospel for years, and it's about time it got put into writing."

Make room for O

Renowned magazine-industry expert and critic Samir Husni, a.k.a. Mr. Magazine, recently compiled this list of notable launches for the month of April 2000. *O: The Oprah Magazine* may be the only one you've seen or heard of, but, as shown below, the magazine-publishing market is a mighty crowded one these days.

Notable magazines launched in April 2000

A

Adoption Today $3.95; 56 pages

B

Bedrooms & Baths: Baths $4.95; 90 p.

Better Homes and Gardens Lightstyle $4.50; 104 p.

Blast Presents Celebrity Scoop $5.95; 52 p.

Boy Next Door Presents Tender Chickens $4.99; 130 p.

C

Celebrity Hairstyles Presents Bridal Star Hairstyles $3.95; 90 p.

Chevy Performance $4.50; 98 p.

D

D Home and Garden $3.95; 96 p.

Dick Berggren's Speedway Illustrated $3.99; 130 p.

Digimon Player Pocket Guide $4.95; 64 p.

DIW Magazine $3.00; 76 p.

DV Web Video $4.95; 64 p.

E

e. Elle supplement 76 p.

eCommerce Business $10.00; 78 p.

Elevation $4.00; 102 p.

F

Fantastic Stories of the Imagination $4.95; 56 p.

Fast & Fun Crochet $2.95; 48 p.

Foliomag.com supplement 32 p.

Foodie Magazine $3.95; 106 p.

G

Good Housekeeping's Best Recipes for Healthy Eating $3.95; 96 p.

H

HX Presents Empire free 98 p.

I

Inside Wrestling Presents Wrestling: The Best of the 20th Century $5.95; 98 p.

K

Krause Publications' Guide to Collecting on the Web $4.99; 460 p.

KUNGFU Qigong Presents Shaolin Temple $4.99; 130 p.

L

Ladies' Home Journal Guide to Women's Health $3.99; 128 p.

Latin CEO $4.95; 96 p.

Laura Ashley Home $9.95; 142 p.

Leg Tease Presents Corporal $7.99; 100 p.

M

Mary Beth's Bean Bag World Special Edition $5.99; 96 p.

Mental Floss free 46 p.

N

Nerve $5.95; 120 p.

New England Travel & Life $3.95; 144 p.

Noon $9.00; 126 p.

O

O: The Oprah Magazine $2.95; 318 p.

P

PC Computing Ziff Davis Smart Business for the New Economy $2.50; 302 p.

PoJo's Collector Card World Digimon $5.95; 112 p.

Pokémon Trading Card Game Player's Guide $14.95; 112 p.

R

Right On Presents Big Pun $3.99; 100 p.

S

Shoot Magazine $5.95; 66 p.

Smart Computing Guide to The Web $5.95; 144 p.

Smart Computing Learning Series PC Tricks $6.95; 144 p.

Soap Opera Update: Soap Stars at Home $9.95; 98 p.

Southern Rodder $3.95; 96 p.

SportFishing Boats $3.95; 112 p.

Sports Illustrated Presents Michigan State Spartans 1999-2000 Champs! $5.95; 88 p.

Sports Illustrated Presents UConn Huskies 1999-2000 Champs! $4.99; 88 p.

Starlog Celebrity Series Presents Teen Love Match $4.99; 48 p.

Street Rod Builder $3.99; 130 p.

Super Rod $3.99; 130 p.

Surfing Girl $2.95; 82p.

T

T Magazine $9.50; 320 p.

Teen Beat All-Stars: *N Sync $3.99; 72 p.

Teen Dream Presents Girls Rule $4.50; 80 p.

The Best of Super Street $4.99; 98 p.

The Game I'll Never Forget $2.50; 66 p.

Time Digital $3.95; 112 p.

Time: Earth Day 2000 $3.95; 96 p.

Todd McFarlane Presents The Crow $4.95; 60 p.

Toxxic Music Series Presents Backstreet Boys Autograph Collector Series $5.95; 52 p.

W

Worldly Remains $4.50; 48 p.

Y

Yellow Rat Bastard $2.95; 114 p.

Oprah's Empire

Strong business sense lands her in rare company

By Andy Dufresne

In the 14 years since the debut of "The Oprah Winfrey Show," Oprah has not only become one of the most successful female entrepreneurs of all time, she has proved to be an integral part of popular culture as well. Talk-show host, publisher, producer, actress, media partner, philanthropist — you name it, Oprah is doing it and doing it extremely well.

From "The Oprah Winfrey Show" — the top-rated talk show 14 years running — to Oprah's Book Club, to her latest venture, *O: The Oprah Magazine*, Oprah has inspired a nation to read better, eat better and live better. And she's done quite well herself, becoming one of the richest African-American women of all time (her current net worth reportedly tops the $725 million mark).

Oprah took her first media-based job at age 19, when she was a student at Tennessee State University in Nashville. Successful gigs in Nashville and Baltimore led Oprah to Chicago, where she took a job opposite the time slot held by then talk-show king Phil Donahue. The show, "A.M. Chicago," quickly skyrocketed to the top of the local Nielson Ratings and was re-launched in 1986 as the nationally syndicated "The Oprah Winfrey Show."

With the first part of her empire in place, Oprah's savvy business sense kicked in and she started acquiring the rest. As the show became an unstoppable force, so did Oprah's entrepreneurial spirit. She quickly established Harpo Productions, Inc., and within a few years she purchased her show from Capital Cities/ABC. "The Oprah Winfrey Show" currently airs in 206 domestic markets and 119 countries worldwide and has opened the door for Oprah to spread her wings financially.

Oprah began driving a harder bargain each time her contract with King World Productions (which syndicated the show nationally) came up for renewal. She is now said to have the best syndication deal in television. By 1988, Harpo Productions compiled enough capital to spend $20 million on the purchase and renovation of a downtown Chicago production facility that then became the company's headquarters. Harpo Productions, Inc. quickly spawned Harpo Films, Inc., Harpo Studios, Inc., and Harpo Video, Inc. This acquisition made Oprah one of only three women in history to own her own television and production studios.

Perhaps the most successful of those ventures is Harpo Films, which inked a long-term contract with ABC Television to produce a series of made-for-television films called *Oprah Winfrey Presents*, which in turn has created such gems as *Before Women Had Wings*; *The Wedding*; *David and Lisa*, and *Tuesdays with Morrie*. Additionally, Oprah has a separate film deal with the Walt Disney Motion Picture Group, the first fruit of which was Touchstone Pictures' 1998 film *Beloved*, in which Oprah also starred. ➜

AP/WIDE WORLD PHOTO

name Oprah the most influential person in the world of books and media in 1997. Her book club was estimated to have fueled the sale of over 12 million books by 1998.

That same year, Oprah partnered with cable veteran Geraldine Laybourne and the independent production team Carsey-Werner-Mandabach to form Oxygen Media, which includes a new women's cable network and the talk-show host's first foray into the Internet. Oxygen's online properties include 19 Web sites such as Thrive, Moms Online, Electra and Oprah Online.

One of the 24-hour Oxygen Network's first television productions is "Oprah Goes Online," a weekly 12-part series offering a step-by-step look at all things online. Although the network is not yet nationwide — large markets like Los Angeles, New York and Chicago have yet to carry the channel — current women's programming leader Lifetime will surely find itself in a heated battle when Oxygen goes big-time. Like all things Oprah, it was the media maven's instincts that told her to get involved with Oxygen.

"I've always made all my decisions based on gut," said Oprah. "My gut told me it was time to leave Baltimore. My gut will tell me whether to continue the (Oprah Winfrey) show or not. And creating a network that has the best interest of women at ➜

Oprah currently occupies the No. 3 spot on the Forbes Celebrity 100, behind actress Julia Roberts and filmmaker George Lucas.

All this wheeling and dealing led to one obvious place by the mid-90s: *Forbes* magazine's coveted lists. In 1993, Oprah topped the magazine's 40 highest-paid entertainers list, a feat she duplicated in 1996 (she has been among the list's top five ever since). But the real coup came in 1995, when Oprah squeezed into *Forbes'* "400 Richest People in America" at No. 399; she now resides at No. 359. Not only was she the only entertainer to make the cut, she was also the only African-American present. She currently occupies the No. 3 spot on the *Forbes* Celebrity 100, behind actress Julia Roberts and filmmaker George Lucas.

While Oprah has clearly made an impact in the film industry, she is widely given credit for single-handedly reviving the publishing industry in 1996. That's when Oprah's Book Club, an on-air reading club, was launched amid a bevy of skepticism on Oprah's part. "I thought we would die in the ratings," she said. "I thought (the producers) had lost their minds."

The book club's inaugural selection, Jacquelyn Mitchard's "The Deep End of the Ocean," shot straight to the top of *The New York Times* Best Seller List, erasing her fears in a heartbeat. Countless subsequent book-club selections have followed suit, prompting *Newsweek* to

AP/WIDE WORLD PHOTO

1999 *Forbes* 400 Richest Americans (Nos. 350 to 400). *Forbes'* Rich List Index by worth in millions

Name	Worth	Age	Source
Saylor, Michael	840	34	Software
Strawbridge, George Jr.	825	61	Inheritance (Campbell Soup)
Milliken, Roger	825	83	Textiles
Shorenstein, Walter Herbert	800	84	Real estate
Hearst, George Randolph Jr.	800	72	Inheritance
Spanos, Alexander Gus	800	77	Real estate
Herb, Marvin J.	800	62	Coca-Cola bottler
Gallo, Ernest	800	90	Wine
Hearst, David Whitmire Jr.	800	54	Inheritance
Cooke, Phoebe Hearst	800	72	Inheritance
Park, Raymond P.	800	73	Manufacturing, real estate
Thorne, Oakleigh Blakeman	800	67	Publishing
Riggio, Leonard	800	58	
Boudjakdji, Millicent V.	800	59	Inheritance
Price, Michael F.	800	48	Money management
Ford, Josephine F.	800	76	Inheritance (Ford Motor Co.)
Lindner, Carl Henry Jr.	800	80	Insurance
Hearst, Austin	800	47	Inheritance
Solow, Sheldon Henry	800	71	Real estate
Cook, Scott D.	780	47	Intuit Inc.
Haas, Peter E. Jr.	775	51	Inheritance (Levi Strauss)
Copley, Helen Kinney	775	76	Media
Liemandt, Joseph A.	770	31	Software
Schuler, Barry	750	46	America Online
Oki, Scott	750	50	Microsoft
Robinson, Jesse Mack	750	76	Banking
Manoogian, Richard Alexander	750	63	Masco Corp.
Davenport, Elizabeth Lupton	750	66	Inheritance (Coca-Cola bottling)
Roberts, Brian L.	750	40	Comcast
Hascoe, Norman	750	70	Semiconductor materials, investments
Milken, Michael Robert	750	53	Junk bonds
Lupton, John Thomas	750	73	Coca-Cola bottling
Adelson, Sheldon	750	66	Trade shows, casinos
Perry, Claire Eugenia Getty	740	45	Inheritance (oil)
Earhart, Anne Catherine Getty	740	47	Inheritance (oil)
Getty, Caroline Marie	740	42	Inheritance (oil)
Krach, Keith, J.	730	42	Ariba
Petersen, Robert Einar	725	73	Publishing
Geballe, Frances Koshland	725	78	Inheritance (Levi Strauss)
Winfrey, Oprah	725	46	Television
Pittman, Robert	725	45	America Online
Haas, Josephine B.	725	85	Inheritance (Levi Strauss)
Katzenberg, Jeffrey	725	48	Entertainment
Magerko, Maggie Hardy	725	33	Lumber
Haas, Evelyn Danzig	720	82	Inheritance (Levi Strauss)
May, Cordelia Scaife	720	71	Inheritance
Kriens, Scott	715	42	Juniper Networks
Lyon, Frank Jr.	700	58	Beverage bottling, investments
Jones, Jerral W.	700	56	Oil and gas
McCormack, Mark	700	68	Sports management

Source: www.forbes.com

Oprah's Empire

The *Forbes* Celebrity 100 is ranked according to annual income and respective amounts of media coverage. The income figure is what the celebrity earned in 1999. The media buzz factor (presence on the web, magazine covers, etc.) is a way of measuring their future earning power.

2000 *Forbes Top 10* Celebrity 100

	Name	Money Rank	Earnings	Web Hits	Press Clips	Magazine Covers	TV and Radio Hits
1	Julia Roberts	12	$50m.	41,131	9,978	7	105
2	George Lucas	1	$400m.	52,199	10,195	1	82
3	Oprah Winfrey	2	$150m.	26,150	9,575	3	103
4	Tom Hanks	5	$71.5m.	43,278	10,141	1	126
5	Michael Jordan	23	$40m.	263,572	38,888	3	267
6	Rolling Stones	11	$50m.	70,999	18,158	0	130
7	Tiger Woods	17	$47m.	85,137	32,974	2	71
8	Backstreet Boys	8	$60m.	49,810	10,157	2	40
9	Cher	25	$40m.	93,670	12,987	3	130
10	Steven Spielberg	9	$60m.	29,564	14,645	0	94

Source: www.forbes.com

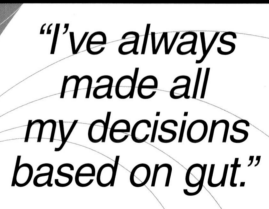

PHOTO BY SHOOTING STAR

"I've always made all my decisions based on gut."

heart — well, that's what I try to do every day. It's such a fit."

All things film and television aside, perhaps Oprah's most ambitious venture to date is *O*, her launch into the fiercely competitive world of magazine publishing. A joint venture between magazine giant Hearst Corporation and the Harpo Entertainment Group, *O* touts itself as a "women's personal-growth guide for the new century." It was launched in April as a bi-monthly title with an initial circulation of 850,000. *O* will be published monthly starting in September, aiming to steal some of the market dominated by the widely popular *Martha Stewart Living*.

O will initially feature its namesake on the cover each month, and in every issue the media magnate writes an opening column, "Let's Talk," and a closing column (inspired by the late movie critic Gene Siskel) called "What I Know For Sure." It's early yet, but if Oprah's track record is any indication, *O* has a bright future ahead of it.

By the end of 2000, Oprah will likely draw closer to becoming America's first black billionaire. In 1999, CBS purchased King World production for $2.5 billion in stock, giving Oprah a one-percent ownership of the network. Although Oprah announced her intention to continue her long-running talk show through 2002, she has since reconsidered.

"It's going to be a huge dilemma," she said. "In the last two seasons I've hit strides in terms of being able to say, more often than not, what I want to say with the shows. It's 200 shows a year — that means 400 more to go. When you think of that, it just sits you down. The question becomes, are there 200 more ways to say what I've already said, on a daily basis? I don't have that answer."

If the past is any guide, legions of loyal fans are eagerly waiting to hear whatever answer Oprah finds. ∎

Andy Dufresne is a freelance writer based in Los Angeles.

1998 Top 40 Entertainers

	Name	1998 Income
1	Jerry Seinfeld	$225 m
2	Larry David	$200 m
3	Steven Spielberg	$175 m
4	Oprah Winfrey	$125 m
5	James Cameron	$115 m
6	Tim Allen	$77 m
7	Michael Crichton	$65 m
8	Harrison Ford	$58 m
9	Rolling Stones	$57 m
10	Master P	$56.5 m
11	Robin Williams	$56 m
12	Celine Dion	$55.5 m
13	Mel Gibson	$55 m
14	Garth Brooks	$54 m
15	Sean (Puffy) Combs	$53.5 m
16	Mike Judge	$53 m
17	Greg Daniels	$53 m
18	Chris Carter	$52 m
19	David Copperfield	$49.5 m
20	Spice girls	$49 m
21	Paul Reiser	$48 m
22	Eddie Murphy	$47.5 m
23	John Travolta	$47 m
24	Drew Carey	$45.5 m
25	Bonnie/Terry Turner	$45 m
26	Tom Hanks	$44 m
27	Danny Jacobson	$42 m
28	Kevin Costner	$41 m
29	Bright/Kauffman/Crane	$40.5 m
30	Brad Pitt	$40 m
31	Stephen King	$40 m
32	Nicolas Cage	$38.5 m
33	Bruce Helford	$38 m
34	Leonardo Dicaprio	$37 m
35	John Wells	$35 m
36	Will Smith	$34 m
37	Jim Carrey	$32.5 m
38	Metallica	$32 m
39	Helen Hunt	$31 m
40	Julia Roberts	$28 m

Source: www.forbes.com

Wise business decisions have helped land Oprah near the top of *Forbes* magazine's lists year after year.

PHOTO BY EVERETT COLLECTION

PHOTO BY EVERETT COLLECTION

Beating the Odds

Oprah overcame more than a few

By Ben Mutzabaugh

This magazine is not officially authorized, approved or endorsed by Oprah Winfrey, Harpo Entertainment Group, or any organization or entity associated or affiliated with Oprah Winfrey.

obstacles *to get to the top*

Oprah Winfrey Tribute

Beating The Odds

PHOTO BY SHOOTING STAR

After struggling for much of her young life, Oprah is enjoying her position as one of the richest, most successful women in America.

There is little question Oprah Winfrey has become one of the most revered celebrities of our time. But while her skills as an actress, host and producer have been widely acknowledged by critics, it is probably her grueling path to fame and fortune that has endeared her to millions of fans.

Born in the poverty and oppressive racial climate of the Deep South in 1954, Oprah was the great-great granddaughter of Constatine and Violet Winfrey, a Mississippi slave couple who was freed after the Civil War. Although Oprah exhibited an exceptional aptitude for learning, she also had a wild and uncontrollable side that forced her to move from relative to relative until she ended up in the custody of her father, a strict disciplinarian.

Despite all the hardships of her childhood, Oprah fused education,

ambition and talent into a vehicle for success as she rose from a position of poverty and a disadvantaged youth to become one of the most successful women in America. Her story is a poignant modern example of living The American Dream, and it has served as an extraordinary source of motivation for women and men throughout the world.

Hard times

Oprah was the child of Vernita Lee, a struggling single mother living deep in the heart of Mississippi at the beginning of the tumultuous Civil Rights Era. Vernita, wary of the poverty and prejudice of the South, decided to make a change. She moved north in hopes of earning better wages while facing fewer social obstacles than she would at home in Mississippi.

While she hoped the North would be more hospitable, Vernita

was worried that bringing along her baby would prove exceedingly difficult. Vernita left Mississippi for Milwaukee in 1954, where she became a housekeeper for affluent white suburban families. But Oprah remained in the South under the care of her grandmother, Hattie Mae Lee.

From the very beginning, Hattie Mae stressed the importance of education to young Oprah, teaching her arithmetic, reading and writing by the age of 3. It also did not take long for Oprah to show a penchant for narrating and performing. Even at her young age, she earned the admiration of church parishioners by performing in plays and reciting biblical passages with remarkable poise and confidence. Likewise, Oprah quickly excelled in school and was advanced directly to first grade after just a few days of kindergarten.

But while Oprah's talents earned her the respect of elders, it also brought rejection by her classmates who resented being "upstaged" by their charismatic peer. As a result, Oprah's years in Mississippi were relatively lonely — with her companionship coming primarily from Hattie Mae and the barnyard animals that lived on her grandmother's farm.

Northward bound

In 1960, at age 6, things changed dramatically for Oprah. With her mother finally established in Milwaukee, Vernita Lee decided it was time for her daughter to join her. The world that Oprah discovered in the North was dramatically different than the one she had become accustomed to in the South. While Vernita was doing better financially in Milwaukee than she had in Mississippi, doing so required that she spend most of the day traveling to and from the distant suburban homes where she cleaned house. This meant little direct supervision of Oprah, who now was forced to share a small one-room apartment with her mother, her mother's boyfriend and a younger child that came out of that relationship.

Oprah no longer was getting the attention she had received at Hattie

Mae's farm. Still, she continued to excel academically, which, just as in Mississippi, earned her the contempt of classmates. Just two years after bringing Oprah to Milwaukee, Vernita Lee again found herself unable to give her daughter the care she deserved. Vernita's live-in boyfriend had reneged on promises to marry, and, desperate for a solution, Vernita called Vernon Winfrey to see if he could help.

Although his identity as such has never been confirmed, Vernon Winfrey is the man that Vernita believed to be Oprah's father. Vernon himself had only learned that he may have fathered the child when he received news clippings of Oprah's birth, along with an ambiguous note from Vernita that read, "Send clothes."

Nonetheless, Vernon and his wife Zelma accepted Oprah into their Nashville home with open arms. Vernon and Zelma were strict guardians, determined to see Oprah live up to her potential. Vernon charged his daughter — now in the third grade — with the task of reading one book per week, with a written book report to follow.

When the next summer came, Oprah boarded a bus back to Milwaukee to visit her mother. Vernita was determined to keep custody of her daughter and refused to let Oprah return to Nashville.

Oprah yearned to return to her father; to a home in which she was the only child of the house and subject to the attention that such a child receives. Back in Milwaukee, she was again thrust into a crowded living situation with her mother and half-sister. Complicating things further were a new live-in boyfriend for Vernita and another child, this time a half-brother for Oprah.

Vernita's crowded apartment also served as a virtual boarding house for various relatives who used it when they had no place else to go. Unfortunately for Oprah, now entering her teen years, this scenario opened the door for one of the most difficult chapters of her life. Oprah has since maintained that several

PHOTO BY SHOOTING STAR

male family members sexually abused her during this time.

About this time, desegregation had begun at schools across the nation. Oprah was accepted into the Upward Bound program, which aimed to bring minorities to predominantly white private schools. With a full scholarship, Oprah began attending an upper middle-class school in suburban Milwaukee. While the school was superior to the rough public school she had attended in the city, the transition was a difficult one. Oprah became acutely aware of the differences between her and her affluent white classmates.

The turmoil at home, coupled with her alienation in the classroom, led Oprah to become increasingly rebellious. She became more difficult for Vernita to handle and finally ran away from home —

➜

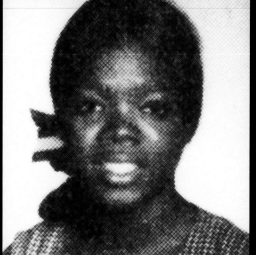

Oprah Timeline:

From her birth to the start of an American success story

1954 — Oprah Winfrey is born on Jan. 29 to Vernita Lee in Kosciusko, Miss. Vernita leaves to find a better life in the North, leaving Oprah with her grandmother, Hattie Mae.

1960 — Oprah leaves Mississippi to join her mother in Milwaukee. A trying time for young Oprah, she is sexually abused by male family members and grapples with feelings of alienation from her peers.

1967 — Becoming increasingly wild and difficult for her mother to handle, Oprah goes to live permanently with Vernon Winfrey in Nashville.

1971 — Oprah hired as a part-time newscaster at WVOL radio in Nashville. That same year, Oprah enrolls as a speech and drama major at Tennessee State University.

1973 — Oprah lands her first full-time media position, going to Nashville CBS Affiliate Channel 5 as the city's first female and first black reporter. She drops out of Tennessee State to accept the position.

1976 — Baltimore ABC affiliate WJZ-TV asks Oprah to join its staff as co-anchor, an impressive position for a 22-year-old. Oprah accepts WJZ's offer but struggles in her new surroundings and is pulled off the anchor desk within nine months.

1978 — Still at WJZ, the station reassigns her to co-host its local talk show, "People Are Talking." Oprah redeems herself as ratings for the show soar, topping even those of talk-show juggernaut Phil Donahue.

1984 — Oprah joins the staff of WLS-TV in Chicago, where she takes over as host of the station's struggling talk show, "A.M. Chicago." The show is renamed "The Oprah Winfrey Show" in 1985.

1985 — Oprah turns in a poignant performance as an actress in *The Color Purple*, taking her celebrity status to a new level. Her performance earns her nominations for an Academy Award and a Golden Globe for Best Supporting Actress.

1986 — "The Oprah Winfrey Show" goes into national syndication. Also, Oprah forms Harpo Productions, Inc., her own production company.

1987 — "The Oprah Winfrey Show" topples "Donahue" as the top-rated talk show in America. The show wins three Daytime Emmy Awards.

1988 — Oprah becomes the first woman in history to own and produce her own talk show after her Harpo Productions assumes ownership and production responsibilities for "The Oprah Winfrey Show."

Despite the hardships, Oprah excelled throughout her childhood. She advanced to the first grade after only a few days of kindergarten; she showed remarkable poise as a public speaker; she was voted the Most Popular Girl by her high school classmates, and she was successful in a number of local beauty pageants.

remaining on the lam for a week before returning home after she ran out of money.

Finding her way

Vernita begrudgingly came to the conclusion that she could not handle Oprah and attempted to enroll her in a halfway house for troubled teens. The home, however, did not have room for Oprah, which turned out to be a blessing. Vernon Winfrey agreed to take Oprah back into his home, where his strict discipline quickly set his daughter back on a path that helped her become the media superstar she is today.

Oprah had to resume her book reports, now up to five every two weeks. She had to obey strict curfews and was told by her father that any grade below an A was not acceptable.

Although it was a marked change from her time with her mother, Oprah began to flourish under her father's tutelage. No longer engaging in a futile search for acceptance, Oprah's academic career took off as well. Now attending a desegregated middle-class school in Nashville, Oprah ➔

Beating The Odds

finally had the respect and admiration of her classmates, culminating in her being named the school's Most Popular Girl during her senior year.

Perhaps beginning to realize the enchantment that she could spin on an audience, Oprah also began competing in beauty pageants. Oprah became very successful in this venture as well, allowing her sense of self-worth to continue to blossom. While her father generally frowned on her participation in pageants, Oprah made it pay off when she won a four-year scholarship to Tennessee State University by winning an Elks Club pageant.

But before she even enrolled at Tennessee State, Oprah found a valuable part-time job with Nashville radio station WVOL, where she spent her senior year reading newscasts after school and on weekends. That job continued as Oprah went to college as a speech and drama major.

After just two years of college, opportunity came knocking. Oprah's part-time gig had gone well at WVOL — so well that it caught the attention

of Nashville's CBS television affiliate, Channel 5. Station directors were looking for minority employees, and they jumped at the chance to lure the talented and dynamic Winfrey to their staff. Of course, accepting the job would mean she would have to drop out of school. Oprah struggled with the difficult decision.

After consulting her father and her professors, Oprah decided to take the chance. And from this humble beginning a broadcasting legend began.

Oprah spent the next three years at Channel 5, where she became Nashville's first black newscaster. Then, at age 22, Oprah's next big career opportunity presented itself. Baltimore ABC affiliate WJZ-TV came calling, asking Oprah to join their staff as a co-anchor. She eagerly accepted, excited about the opportunity of such a prestigious post in such a large East Coast market. But the honeymoon didn't last long. She found herself at odds with bosses and co-workers, who pushed a restrictive agenda that Oprah wasn't accustomed to. After having a relatively free reign at Channel 5, Oprah struggled to adapt to WJZ's more conservative approach.

Shackled by WJZ's rigid guidelines — which ranged from how to style her hair to not allowing her to ad-lib during newscasts — Oprah lasted only nine months before station managers pulled her off the anchor desk. Humiliated, Oprah fell into a deep depression and became plagued by self doubt. But in those moments of deep despair came the opportunity that launched her career onto a path of fame and stardom.

Oprah had agreed to a six-year contract with WJZ, so while the station had yanked her from the anchor desk, firing her was not a realistic option. Instead, WJZ tabbed Oprah to co-host its local morning talk show, "People Are Talking." The show aired opposite Phil Donahue's popular talk show, which dominated the ratings in that time slot. Most at the station believed Oprah and the show

would bomb, but there was nothing to lose with Donahue already controlling the time slot.

Then the impossible happened: "People Are Talking" outdid "Donahue."

Freed from the anchor desk's oppression, Oprah began to thrive on the spontaneity and her command of the audience that made her so successful in Nashville. She established a natural camaraderie with the show's guests, and she always seemed to ask the question her audience was begging for. It was a natural fit. Oprah made the show a success.

"People Are Talking" continued to win its time slot in Baltimore and word of Oprah and her success gradually spread to television executives around the country. At 29 and in her seventh year in Baltimore, Oprah had done about all she could as co-host of a talk show. And again, her next big opportunity would come calling.

Star quality

In January 1984, Winfrey was lured to Chicago by WLS-TV to host "A.M. Chicago," that station's struggling morning talk show. There, she found herself pitted against the formidable "Donahue" show one more time. And again, few media pundits forecasted success for Oprah.

What happened next shocked the entertainment world. Now as host of her own show, Oprah again whipped "Donahue" — this time in the nation's third-largest television market. Just 12 weeks after debuting in Chicago, she had put an end to a 16-year run by "Donahue" as the highest-rated talk show host there. Her ascension to the top was nothing short of remarkable, and Oprah was drawing national attention. In fact, her performances on "A.M. Chicago" eventually attracted the casting staff of the 1985 Steven Spielberg film, *The Color Purple*.

Oprah immediately was pegged for the role of Sofia, a strong-willed black woman who suffered through abusive relationships with men. Oprah strongly identified with the part and said it was "the happiest day of my life" when she was picked for the character. Although inexperienced as an actress, she delivered a stunning and impassioned performance as Sofia, one that earned her an Oscar nomination for Best Supporting Actress.

That cemented Oprah as a household name in America. It was, perhaps, the most remarkable chapter in the stunning transformation from her roots as a troubled child initially raised by her grandmother on a pig farm in rural Mississippi to a glamorous, nationally known entertainer. Now Oprah was on everybody's television and on every celebrity's guest list.

Her success continued to grow even after *The Color Purple*. Winfrey again received critical acclaim for her role in a second movie — *Native Son* — while her talk show continued to surpass all expectations.

In September 1985, the ratings juggernaut "A.M. Chicago" was renamed "The Oprah Winfrey Show." The show went national on Sept. 8, 1986 and became the number-one talk show in national syndication in less than a year, receiving three Daytime Emmy Awards in its first year of eligibility.

In October 1988, Oprah again raised the bar when her own Harpo Productions, Inc. assumed ownership and all production responsibilities for the show, making Oprah the first woman in history to own and produce her own talk show.

PHOTO BY SHOOTING STAR

Oprah's rise from poverty and oppression in the South to one of the wealthiest and most powerful women in the world is unprecedented in our time. And, with Oprah continually building on her status as an entertainment mogul in the new millennium, her remarkable journey stands to cover new and higher ground in the years ahead. ∎

Ben Mutzabaugh is a Chicago-based freelance writer.

From her phenomenal debut in *The Color Purple* to the tumultuous 10-year battle she fought to bring *Beloved* to the big screen, follow Oprah Winfrey's film career from her earliest acting aspirations to her current position among the ranks of Hollywood's elite

Leading Lady

By **Michelle Mulder**

AP/WIDE WORLD PHOTO

Oprah poses with Steven Spielberg, who directed her in *The Color Purple*.

L ike most young girls at some point in their lives, Oprah Winfrey often dreamed about becoming an actress, of seeing herself larger-than-life on the silver screen. She wanted to try on other people's lives, to share their triumphs and tragedies and to utter words that were not her own, because, as she says now, it is the "ultimate in understanding."

And to a certain extent, she lived out some of this film-star fantasy from an early age, mostly by performing as an orator in her church and for her family.

Oprah was reciting in church by age 3, and by age 7 she had graduated to bible verses and poetry, like "Invictus" by William Ernest Henley, even though she didn't fully understand what she was reciting. All she knew ➔

was that by saying it, she seemed to be showered with special attention. "People would say, 'Whew, that child can speak!' " she later recalled.

So Oprah turned her gift for gab into a promising career in broadcasting and set aside her acting aspirations for a while. But, she admits the desire to act continued to burn inside her for many years. "I always wanted to be an actress for most of my adolescent and adult life," she said.

However, her strict father's disapproval of acting as a realistic career choice kept her from following that passion — at first. "His idea of an actress was one of these 'lewd women,' " said Oprah. Ultimately, Oprah couldn't tempt fate any longer and she managed, albeit in a roundabout way, to set the stage for her future film career with the help of one man.

"I read the first page of the book, put it down and wept."

The chance of a lifetime

Hollywood tales about average folks being discovered while waiting tables or shopping in the local grocery store are legendary. But the fact is, this happens to very few people. With thousands of very talented, aspiring actors and actresses competing for the same roles, it's practically unheard of for an unknown to sweep in under Hollywood radar and steal a coveted film role. But that's exactly what happened in Oprah's case.

"Quincy Jones discovered me," she said. "He was in his hotel room and saw me on TV. It was unbelievable."

As it turned out, Quincy saw Oprah on a local broadcast when she was hosting a morning talk ➡

After seeing a local broadcast of Oprah's morning talk show, Quincy Jones recommended her to Steven Spielberg. This led to Oprah securing the role of Sofia in *The Color Purple*.

The Color Purple **1985**

AP/WIDE WORLD PHOTO

Brewster Place 1990

Oprah Winfrey Tribute

There Are No Children Here 1993

AP/WIDE WORLD PHOTO

Despite the demands associated with an acting career, Oprah has continued to host her syndicated talk show.

show in Chicago, and immediately thought she'd be a good fit for his upcoming project with Steven Spielberg. And so, from out of nowhere, Oprah landed the role of Sofia in *The Color Purple* (1985).

An adaptation of Alice Walker's best-selling novel, *The Color Purple* is the moving tale of a young black girl in the South who rises from tragedy to triumph over the course of 40 years. Even before she won a role in the movie, Oprah was won over by the book. "I read the first page of the book, put it down and wept," said Oprah. "I could not believe it, that someone had put this in writing."

The novel and the movie, mostly about how women survive in a male-dominated culture, also dealt with the topic of sexual abuse, a subject with which Oprah could easily relate since she had been abused in her own childhood. This ability to connect with the story and the characters helped Oprah greatly with her debut role. Along with costars Whoopi Goldberg, Danny Glover and Margaret Avery, Oprah turned in an emotionally gripping performance that earned her an Oscar nomination and a Golden Globe nomination for Best Supporting Actress — a remarkable achievement for any actress, particularly a newcomer.

Her role in *The Color Purple* had an immense effect on Oprah's career, catapulting her to superstardom with a single effort. The success of the film opened many doors for Oprah, including setting into motion

the events that led to her assuming the role of host of a nationally televised program, "The Oprah Winfrey Show." The television program quickly gained a devoted following and ensured Oprah's place in the culture and consciousness of America.

The film also had a profound influence on Oprah the person, especially the scene that she calls the most powerful in the movie.

In it, her character, Sofia, is walking through a cornfield and proclaims herself to Celie (played by

Beloved 1998

AP/WIDE WORLD PHOTO

Oprah both starred in and produced *Beloved*, based on the novel by Toni Morrison.

Goldberg). "She says, 'All my life I had to fight. I had to fight my cousins. I had to fight my brothers. I had to fight my uncles. But I ain't never thought I had to fight my own house.' I did that scene in one take because it was the essence, I thought, of my life," said Oprah.

"I did that scene in one take because it was the essence, I thought, of my life."

"She was saying, 'I'm not going to fight people anymore. I'm going to have what I deserve.' It's taken me a while to get to where Sofia was, but it was so liberating."

Her acting ambition free at last, Oprah the aspiring actress enjoyed what would be a breakthrough year in 1985. With both the Oscar and Golden Globe nominations on her resume, she also was listed as one of the 12 "Most Promising Actors" in John Willis' *Screen World* magazine. She then earned her next role as Mrs. Thomas in *Native Son* (1986) with Geraldine Page and Matt Dillon. ➜

Beloved 1998

All through her life, despite her father's early objections, Oprah craved the challenges of acting.

Oprah would follow that project with her role as LaJoe Rivers in the TV movie *There Are No Children Here* (1993), which was filmed in Chicago's Henry Horner Projects and helped turn attention to the perils of at-risk inner-city youth. At about this time it became clear that Oprah, despite her father's objections early on, was a bona fide actress.

But she also was starting to realize that it just might not be enough to be on the big screen. Now, Oprah wanted to be calling the shots behind the camera as well.

Master of her own destiny

In the midst of all the Hollywood hoopla surrounding Oprah's burgeoning acting career, she still continued to meet the daily demands of hosting her nationally syndicated talk show. She quickly realized she couldn't continue juggling the demands of acting and hosting her show if she had to bow to the restrictions imposed by others. Plus, she rationalized, why work

Beloved 1998

AP/WIDE WORLD PHOTO

Oprah, with Danny Glover, portrayed Sethe, a former slave, in the movie *Beloved*. The story takes place shortly after the Emancipation.

Oprah Winfrey Filmography

Actress
- *Beloved* (1998)
- *Oprah Winfrey Presents: Before Women Had Wings* (1997) (TV movie)
- *About Us: The Dignity of Children* (1997) (TV special)
- *There Are No Children Here* (1993) (TV movie)
- *Lincoln* (1992) (TV series) (voice)
- *Listen Up: The Lives of Quincy Jones* (1990)
- *Brewster Place* (1990) (TV series)
- *The Women of Brewster Place* (1989) (TV movie)
- *Throw Momma from the Train* (1987)
- *Native Son* (1986)
- *The Color Purple* (1985)

Producer
- *Oprah Winfrey Presents: Tuesdays with Morrie* (1999) (TV movie)
- *Oprah Winfrey Presents: David and Lisa* (1998) (TV movie)
- *Beloved* (1998)
- *Oprah Winfrey Presents: The Wedding* (1998) (TV movie)
- *Oprah Winfrey Presents: Before Women Had Wings* (1997) (TV movie)
- *Overexposed* (1992) (TV movie)
- *Overexposed* (1990)
- *The Women of Brewster Place* (1989) (TV movie)
- *The Oprah Winfrey Show* (1986) (TV talk show)

Beloved 1998

AP/WIDE WORLD PHOTO

During the filming of *Beloved*, Oprah created an altar in her trailer where she would put the names collected from slave ledgers along with the prices that were paid for them at the slave auctions.

Beloved 1998

AP/WIDE WORLD PHOTO

for someone else when you have the opportunity and the resources to work for yourself, to control your own show?

So she set out on yet another ambitious project. She created Harpo Productions, Inc. (Harpo is Oprah spelled backwards), which encompasses Harpo Films, Inc. and Harpo Videos, Inc. She also built Harpo Studios, a $20 million complex in downtown Chicago which boasts a TV studio for her show and three movie soundstages. By doing so, Oprah became only the third woman in history — after Mary Pickford and Lucille Ball — and the first African-American, to own a major studio. "The studio came about as a result of me wanting more time and creativity, and control in myself," said Oprah. "I bought the studio so I would be able to act and do the show at the same time."

It also allowed Oprah the freedom to step into a new role as producer. "What I really want to do is create films, for myself and other people, that uplift, enlighten, encourage and entertain," she said. Her first producing effort, the TV miniseries *The Women of Brewster Place* (1989), was successful enough ➜

to become a short-lived TV series the following year.

In addition to serving as executive producer, Oprah starred as Mattie Michael and surrounded herself with a stellar cast of other talented women, including Cicely Tyson; Robin Givens; Jackee Kelly; Paula Kelly; Olivia Cole, Lonette McKee and Jackee. The TV movie marked a significant step in Oprah's career because it was the first time she was able to use her clout as a star to produce. And by telling the stories of a group of black women living in an inner-city brownstone, she was fulfilling her dream of bringing a realistic portrayal of the African-American experience to the small screen.

Both critics and TV executives were impressed with her efforts. ABC offered her a deal to provide prime-time programming under the Oprah Winfrey Presents name. "We have a thorough trust in Oprah

Although not a smash hit, the fact that *Beloved* even made it to the big screen is a testament to the power that Oprah wields in the industry.

"I felt when I read this book that I was Sethe and Sethe was me."

and her instincts," ABC president Robert A. Iger said at the time. "If she has something she wants to make, we'll let her." And after inking another deal, a multi-picture contract with Disney, Oprah was well on her way to achieving her latest set of filmmaking goals. Throughout the '90s, she would embark on a slew of projects for both the small and big screen.

A dream fulfilled

As part of her deal with Disney, Oprah starred in and produced *Beloved* (1998), based on Toni Morrison's Pulitzer Prize-winning novel about a woman haunted by the baby she murdered and the legacy of slavery. Perhaps most importantly, it was the

Beloved 1998

Beloved 1998

Oprah has said that "*Beloved* really does embody the spirit of our ancestors."

culmination of a 10-year battle to bring this best-seller to the big screen. It proved such a moving experience that it brought her to tears. "I felt I had to tell it," said Oprah. "But, if I had known it was going to take this long I probably would have made another decision."

Just what was it about the story of *Beloved* that attracted Oprah? Much like *The Color Purple*, Oprah first identified with the book and its main character, Sethe, whom she would eventually play in the movie. "I felt when I read this book that I was Sethe and Sethe was me," she said. "We were all connected somehow. I was also stunned, numbed and overwhelmed but didn't really know how to articulate what I was feeling."

Since Sethe is a former slave and the story takes place shortly after the Emancipation, a great deal of the film's focus is on the cultural significance of slavery. Oprah found herself turning to that legacy for inspiration during filming. "*Beloved* really does embody the spirit of our ancestors," she said. "Everyone, not just those whose ancestors were brought to this country as slaves, anyone who had to pay the price and face challenges like learning a new language, finding security and building a future."

In fact, Oprah created an altar in her trailer where she would put names she'd gotten from slave ledgers along with the prices that had been paid for them. Each day she would remind herself that she was doing this for Big John or for Little Anna, 7 years old and $350.

For *Beloved*, Oprah teamed up once again with her former *Color Purple* co-star, Danny Glover. She also faced her greatest on-screen challenge: her first love scene. Oprah admits she was terrified. "I didn't find out until afterward that Danny had never done a love scene, either," she said. "I wish he'd told me because I was a wreck that day."

She recalled that director Jonathan Demme actually pulled her aside and told her to relax and think about how great it would be to kiss Danny Glover, especially since it wasn't even her, it was Sethe. But, replied Oprah, "She's using my body and lips!"

Although it was not considered a box-office blockbuster, the fact that *Beloved* was even produced is a true credit to Oprah's power in Hollywood. That year, *Entertainment Weekly* ranked her first on its annual list of the 101 most influential people in Hollywood.

So, what lies ahead for Oprah's movie-making career? The decision is hers, depending on how much time she chooses to devote to acting in and producing films as compared with continuing her talk show, publishing her magazine and various other pursuits. Other movie projects and plum roles are certain to come along, and the ones she ultimately pursues will get the full range of her talents and will require much of her valuable time.

Whatever Oprah decides to do in terms of continuing to create and produce quality entertainment, this much is certain: If there is a story to tell, she will see that it's told. ■

Michelle Mulder is a freelance writer based in Los Angeles.

AP/WIDE WORLD PHOTO

Love of her Life

Grounded Graham provides steadying influence

By Jim Shevis

Oprah Winfrey is one of those people who seems to have known early in life where she was going. At age 12, while visiting her father in Nashville, Winfrey was paid $500 to speak at a church. "I told my daddy then and there that I planned to be very famous," she said. "I wanted to be paid to talk."

That she reached her goal is self-evident. "The Oprah Winfrey Show" has made her a household name and one of the highest-paid entertainers in the world. She has everything money can buy: a condo on Chicago's Gold Coast, a ranch in Telluride, Colo., an oceanside dwelling in Miami and much more.

But for much of her life, she lacked what money couldn't buy: the happiness that a loving, trusting relationship can bring. She lacked a soul mate, someone who would be there when she needed him, through good times and bad.

Oprah had just about given up hope of ever finding Mr. Right when she found him in the 6-foot-6 presence of Stedman Graham Jr. Her life hasn't been the same since. "I think what happened is what I read about in all the women's magazines," she told ABC's Barbara Walters. "They say if you stop looking, you can find it."

A natural fit

From everything Oprah has said about Graham, her "significant other" since 1986, the Chicago businessman has been a steadying influence and a perfect complement for her. "He is one of the kindest and most patient men I have ever known," she said,

which is "one of the reasons we're still together. And he is honorable. Like my father, just honorable."

Psychologists might look at Graham as a father figure, reminding Oprah of her father, Vernon Winfrey, who kept her on the straight and narrow during her formative years. They might also note with interest that she and Graham have never married, even though they've been together for 15 years. "We'll get married when both of us are ready," Oprah has said often.

Who is this Stedman Graham Jr., this rock of support for the nation's No. 1 talk-show host? What do they have in common? For starters, they share similar interests and beliefs. They're both shrewd business people. Both are positive-minded, exponents of the human-potential movement.

Oprah Wi...

Oprah and Graham's 15-year romance was almost over before it began, as she stood him up on what would have been their first date in 1985. Fortunately, he persisted.

Graham has been highly successful in business. He is president and CEO of Stedman Graham & Associates, a Chicago-based sports-management, marketing and consulting firm. He is also the founder of Athletes Against Drugs, a non-profit organization created to combat substance abuse and to promote youth leadership. In his spare time, he wrote a *New York Times* Best Seller ("You Can Make It Happen: A Nine-Step Plan for Success") that he dedicated to Oprah.

"Without her influence and her belief in me, I doubt that I ever would have discovered true freedom and what it means," Graham revealed. "Her knowledge and understanding of the world has added so much to my life. I shall always be grateful to her for helping to fill the hole in my heart."

Graham is three years older than Oprah. Born in 1951 in Whitesboro, N.J., an African-American community surrounded by a predominantly white county, he was one of six children, two of whom were developmentally disabled. Their father was a painter and contractor, their mother a homemaker.

Because of his height and prowess as a basketball player, Graham starred on his high school team. His athletic skills enabled him to get a college education. He earned a Bachelor of Arts degree in social work at Hardin-Simmons University in Texas and a master's degree in education at Ball State University in Indiana.

Basketball was his passion; he dreamed of playing professionally. But, he has said, he lacked the self-esteem and support he needed to go for it.

He married shortly after he graduated from Hardin-Simmons in 1974. The following year, he became a father when his daughter Wendy was born. He and his wife later divorced. Some say he has been marriage-shy ever since and that this explains why he and Oprah have yet to tie the knot.

He played basketball in Europe for three years, averaging 30 points a game, but was unable to break into the National Basketball Association — one of the biggest disappointments in his life. Sports remained a big part of Stedman's life, however. In addition to founding Athletes Against Drugs and Stedman Graham & Associates, he wrote a column for *Inside Sports* magazine. In 1994, he was named director of George Washington University's Forum for Sport and Event Management and Marketing in Washington, D.C.

His own man

Graham's romance with Oprah began in 1985. Cautious at first because of doubts about herself, Oprah stood him up. But after he called again, she went out with him. As time went on, their relationship blossomed.

"Stedman is ideal for me," she said. "He's my No. 1 fan, and he isn't jealous of my success."

In an interview with *Essence* magazine, Oprah said, "He knows who he is. I am thrilled that I have discovered this in a black man."

Graham's willingness to stay out of the limelight is an indication of his independence and his inner security. But it hasn't always been easy being the boyfriend of a megastar, as Graham acknowledged in a first-person article in the March 1997 issue of *McCall's*. One day, as he was walking along a Chicago street, a construction worker greeted him with,"Hey, Oprah's boyfriend, how's it going?"

At one time, being seen only as Oprah Winfrey's boyfriend might have made him flinch and give the worker a cold stare, said Graham. But because he had overcome the low self-esteem and negative racial images of his youth, he let the remark pass. Instead, he shook the man's hand and struck up a conversation. "At the end of our conversation, he called me Mr. Graham," he said, an altogether healthier title than the "Mr. Oprah" title others had given him.

Graham believes his relationship with Oprah was the catalyst to gaining a better understanding of himself. As Oprah became a national celebrity, Graham couldn't avoid feeling increasingly uncomfortable.

"I was an unequal partner, at least in the eyes of the public," he said. "The pain of dealing with this issue forced me to look inside myself."

But without Oprah's help and

continued on p.75

Love of her Life

Oprah Winfrey

PHOTO BY GLOBE

PHOTO BY SHOOTING STAR

PHOTO BY SHOOTING STAR

Heads of the Class

No one would accuse Oprah of being afraid to accept new challenges. In September 1999, she further expanded her repertoire by taking on the role of professor, as she and her long-time companion, Stedman Graham, jointly taught a class at Northwestern University's Kellogg Graduate School of Management in Evanston, Ill.

The class, "The Dynamics of Leadership," was offered to 100 second-year business school students, but six hundred competed in an Internet registration, with spots going to the highest bidders. (Kellogg students receive 3,000 points to bid with each year, to be doled out over a year's worth of courses.)

The talk-show host had culled considerable interest from Kellogg's graduate students, particularly because of her regular appearances at or near the top of the *Forbes* Top 40 entertainers list. As for Oprah, the opportunity to be a professor allowed her to achieve her dream to teach.

"I jumped at the opportunity," Oprah said. Graham, on the other hand, had already had plenty of experience in lecturing, having conducted a sports-marketing class at Northwestern prior to "Dynamics of Leadership."

Rich Honack, Assistant Dean and Director of Marketing and Communications at Kellogg, said the emphasis of the class was definitely on business, not entertainment.

"Students looked at this as a businesswoman coming in to teach, to tell students that when they're in business, they are in charge of their own destinies," said Honack.

Love of her Life

Though an extremely successful businessman in his own right, Graham was thrust into the spotlight as Oprah's career skyrocketed.

understanding, Graham might not have come to realize what had been holding him back from a fuller life.

"Oprah forced me to confront my insecurities," he said. "She tried to make me understand that the roots of my pain were in my past. I stewed over her words for a long time before I acknowledged she was right."

The 'M' word

Interestingly, Graham did not discuss the oft-broached matter of marrying Oprah in the *McCall's* piece. For her part, Oprah has said she's "sick, sick, sick" of the question.

In 1997, when the couple was interviewed on "The Gayle King Show," members of the audience posed the marriage question to them.

Graham, first engaged to Winfrey in 1992, had joined King in her Hartford, Conn., studio while

Winfrey joined them by satellite from Chicago. The 1997 interview marked the first time the couple had been interviewed on a talk show together. Winfrey replied that they had no immediate plans to take the plunge.

"I think we have a deep love and caring for each other, and respect," she said. "Every day we get asked a question about when we're getting married, and I say it works so well the way it is, I wouldn't want to mess it up.

"I think that for us, this is what works right now, which is not to say that we never would get married."

Oprah said that what makes her and Graham's relationship work is honesty and the commitment they have for each other. "He is one person who would tell me the truth... and I would tell him the truth."

Of her long-time friend King, Oprah says, "She keeps me

grounded." And Graham encourages the friendship: "I think it's therapeutic for Oprah to have someone she can talk to and tell everything about her day and everything about her week."

Besides Graham and King, Oprah's inner circle includes her attorney, Jeffrey Jacobs, who has guided her career; Bill and Camille Cosby; Barbara Walters; composer and producer Quincy Jones, and author Maya Angelou.

Because of their ever-full schedules, Graham and Winfrey share a long-distance romance. Yet they find ways to stay in touch. Together, in the fall of 1999, they taught a course in leadership at Northwestern University's Kellogg Graduate School of Management. The course, "Dynamics of Leadership," which they developed jointly, was designed to help business students enhance their abilities to lead effectively. →

Graham's definition of ethical leadership is "consistency over time in matters such as honesty and hard work, and setting a good example," a code that Oprah embraces as well.

For a while in 1994, there was talk that Oprah, the highest-paid daytime TV talk-show host in America, might leave television to take on new challenges. Since then, she has branched out into producing films and TV specials, launched an on-air book club, a women's magazine and still is hosting the show.

For someone this busy, it's hard to imagine there's also room for marriage. But if there's to be one, Graham is the more-than-likely candidate. He's a success in his own right, secure enough to live with the incandescent Oprah and still be his own man. ∎

Jim Shevis is a freelance writer based in Washington, D.C.

Love of her Life

"Stedman is ideal for me," Oprah says of her companion. "He knows who he is."

What if . . .

Everybody knows that Oprah and her steady, Stedman Graham, have been a tight couple for years. While their relationship is strong as ever, it's interesting, and perhaps entertaining, to think of how things may have turned out if Oprah's man were another ultra-famous (or infamous) individual. Gold Collectors Series has compiled a list of spoof suitors to see how the course of history (or covers of tabloids) may have been altered had Oprah chosen someone with a fame quotient even higher than the demure Mr. Graham.

AP/WIDE WORLD PHOTO

David Letterman

The late-night host has served up a steady diet of Oprah jokes over the years, notably bombing as Oscars host as a result. But perhaps heart bypass surgery has uncovered a softer side of Dave that Oprah might find more tolerable.

Bill Gates

The billionaire software mogul would have an open forum to be consoled on a daily basis, with the recent antitrust decision threatening a break-up of his Microsoft baby. With their gargantuan fortunes combined, Harpo Studios could also have the funding to relocate to its own country.

AP./WIDE WORLD PHOTO

Michael Jordan

The ultimate Mr. and Mrs. Icon, this star-power couple could be the true rags-to-riches duo. Both were from modest, Southern upbringings and shot to international illuminati status as Chicagoans.

AP/WIDE WORLD PHOTO

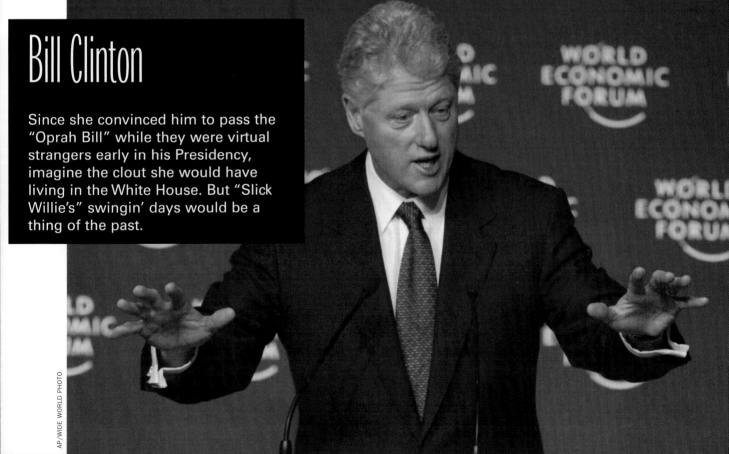

Bill Clinton

Since she convinced him to pass the "Oprah Bill" while they were virtual strangers early in his Presidency, imagine the clout she would have living in the White House. But "Slick Willie's" swingin' days would be a thing of the past.

AP/WIDE WORLD PHOTO

Michael Jackson

His infatuation with Diana Ross is well-documented, if not only in the tabloids certainly in his ever-changing appearance. Who's to say Michael won't do an "about-face" and pay tribute to Oprah by presenting a photo of her mug at his next plastic surgery appointment?

Bill Cosby

This pairing truly would have given us a king and queen of television, and together they would have ruled the airwaves. Just consider some of their collaborations: *Oprah Winfrey Presents: Fat Albert and the Cosby Kids* or *Children of Divorce Say the Darndest Things*

Jayson Williams

The NBA star looked downright smitten with Oprah when he appeared on her show in April, and he writes in his new autobiography: "I've always had a thing for Oprah. Oprah fascinates me. Yeah, I can see me and Oprah."

AP/WIDE WORLD PHOTO

Mick Jagger

No more "bad boys of rock 'n' roll" behavior for this aging Stone...and no more nickel tips, either. Waiters and others in the service industry would no longer be under Mick's thumb, and Oprah would no doubt be wearing the pants "When the Whip Comes Down."

AP/WIDE WORLD PHOTO

Oprah's long-time engagement to sports-marketing entrepreneur Stedman Graham is well-known, but several other friends also form her tight inner circle. And because being the ruler of all media can be a daunting task, she needs a strong support system filled wi reliable confidants. Oprah's entourage is comprised of fellow celebrities, long-time acquai tances, a personal trainer, a personal chef and even two canine companions, to name a few. Most of all, it's comprised of people who make a difference in her life.

Gayle King

You can't draft a list of Oprah's allies without including best friend Gayle King, the former TV news anchor, talk-show host and current *O* editor at large. A true testament to their friendship, Oprah purchased a million-dollar home for King.

Quincy Jones

The famed producer and composer, co-producing a film version of Alice Walker's novel "A Color Purple" in 1984, caught a glimpse of Oprah hosting her local talk show, "A.M. Chicago." Jones liked what he saw and suggested Oprah for the role of Sofia. Director Steven Spielberg agreed, and Oprah got the part. She later received a Best Supporting Actress Oscar nomination for her performance, and "O" and "Q" have been tight ever since.

Maya Angelou

Perhaps they're such good friends because they have so much in common. Like Oprah, Angelou is constantly tackling new projects. In addition to her success as a best selling author and poet, she is an accomplished historian, actress, playwright, civil-righ activist, producer and director.

Toni Morrison

Holding a high place in Oprah's heart and on her list of book-club recommendation the author has received countless literary honors, including the 1993 Nobel Prize in Literature.

Bill and Camille Cosby

The ultra-successful Hollywood star and his significant other can relate to Oprah's celebrity status. Cosby's children's books, "The Meanest Thing to Say," "The Treasure Hunt," and "The Best Way to Play," have appeared on Oprah's Book Club lists.

Jeffrey Jacobs

Being Oprah's attorney is a full-time job, and Mr. Jacobs has proved his worth as both a friend and legal representative.

Bob Greene

Prior to making Greene her personal trainer, Oprah's weight problems resembled a bad roller-coaster ride. But Greene's support and sound training regimen have brought stability to Oprah's physical health.

Rosie Daley

Like Greene, Daley plays a huge role in promoting Oprah's physical and mental health. The talented chef ha won a place in her heart (and stomach) by preparing her meals and keeping tabs on her diet.

Sophie and Solomon

Keeping up with your cocker spaniels is extremely difficult for someone who travels as much as Oprah, but she always manages to throw (or send) a bone to her beloved companions.

Toni Morrison and Oprah

Oprah Winfrey Tribute

Out With Oprah

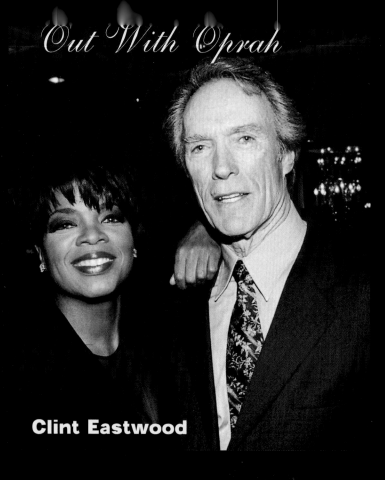

Clint Eastwood

Rosie O'Donnell

Denzel Washington

Candace Bergen

Barbara Walters

Out With Oprah

Jessye Norman

Rehearsal for the 1993 Inauguration

Will Smith
and Jada Pinkett

Martha Stewart

You go, girl!

In her career as a media magnate and through all of her philanthropic pursuits, Oprah has achieved in her 46 years what few people could achieve in 46 lifetimes. Listed below are just some of her most notable and outstanding accomplishments:

2000

- Received the King Center "Salute to Greatness Award"
- Launched *O: The Oprah Magazine*

1999

- Earned National Book Award's 50th Anniversary Gold Medal
- Named to Blackwell's Best-Dressed Women list
- Ranked 3rd on the *Forbes* Celebrity 100 list
- Produced made-for-TV movie, *Tuesdays with Morrie*
- Gained one-percent ownership of CBS
- Rose to No. 359 on the *Forbes* Richest People in America list

1998

- Won NAACP Image Award for Best Actress (for her role in *Beloved)*
- Won Daytime Emmy Award for Best Talk Show Host
- Won People's Choice Award for Favorite Female Television Performer
- Won the National Academy of Television Arts & Sciences' Lifetime Achievement Award
- Produced made-for-TV movie, *The Wedding*
- Voted the Most Powerful Person in the Entertainment Industry
- *Time* magazine named her one of the most influential people of the century
- Partnered with two other parties to form multi-media company Oxygen Media

1997

- Began Oprah's Angel Network to raise money and support for less fortunate members of society
- Won People's Choice Award for Favorite Female Television Performer
- Won Daytime Emmy Award for Best Talk Show
- Won NAACP Image Award for Outstanding News, Talk or Informational Special
- Won NAACP Image Award for Outstanding News, Talk or Informational Series
- Produced made-for-TV movie, *Before Women Had Wings*

1996

- Won Daytime Emmy Award for Best Talk Show
- Topped *Forbes* Highest Paid Entertainers list
- Received the George Foster Peabody Individual Achievement Award
- Won the International Radio and Television Society's Gold Medal Award
- Started Oprah's Book Club

1995

- Ranked No. 399 on *Forbes* Richest People in America list
- Won Daytime Emmy Award for Outstanding Talk/Service Show
- Won Daytime Emmy Award for Outstanding Talk/Service Show Host
- Ran the Marine Corps Marathon in Washington, D.C.

1994

- Won Daytime Emmy Award for Outstanding Talk/Service Show
- Won Daytime Emmy Award for Outstanding Talk/Service Show Host

1993

- Topped *Forbes* Highest Paid Entertainers list for first time
- Won Daytime Emmy Award for Outstanding Talk/Service Show Host
- Won Daytime Emmy Award for Outstanding Children's Special

1992

- Won Daytime Emmy Award for Outstanding Talk/Service Show
- Won Daytime Emmy Award for Outstanding Talk/Service Show Host

1991

- Spoke before Congress to help initiate the Child Protection Act, popularly referred to as "The Oprah Bill." Bill was signed into law in 1993.
- Won Daytime Emmy Award for Outstanding Talk/Service Show
- Won Daytime Emmy Award for Outstanding Talk/Service Show Host

1990

- Hosted the 17th Annual Daytime Emmy Awards

1989

- Won Daytime Emmy Award for Outstanding Talk/Service Show

You go, girl!

1988

- Won Broadcaster of the Year Award from the International Radio and Television Society, (youngest recipient)
- Opened her own television studio, Harpo Productions, Inc.

1987

- Hosted the 14th Annual Daytime Emmy Awards
- Won Daytime Emmy Award for Outstanding Talk/Service Show Host

1986

- Received Academy Award Nomination for Best Supporting Actress (*The Color Purple*)
- "The Oprah Winfrey Show" went into national syndication
- Played the role of "Mrs. Thomas" in *Native Son*

1971

- Named Miss Black Nashville and Miss Black Tennessee

Quotables

PHOTO BY HUTCHINS

"I feel like I would do this if I didn't get a dime for it...because it doesn't even feel like work."

"The greatest thing about what I do, for me, is that I'm in a position to change people's lives."

"It is the most incredible platform for influence that you could imagine, and it's something that I hold in great esteem and take full responsibility for."

"...my intention is always, regardless of what the show is — whether it's about sibling rivalry or wife battering or children of divorce — for people to see within each show that you are responsible for your life, that although there may be tragedy in your life, there's always a possibility to triumph."

"I was in the middle of a show with some white-supremacist skinheads, Ku Klux Klan members, and in the middle of that show, I just had a flash, I thought, 'This is doing nobody any good, nobody.' And I had rationalized the show by saying, 'Oh, people need to know that these kinds of people are out here.' I won't do it anymore."

"I taped a show for a guy who was a mass murderer. He killed eight people. I did the whole interview, and I had the families of some of the people he killed. In the middle of it, flash, I thought, 'I shouldn't be doing this; this is not going to help anybody. It's a voyeuristic look at a serial killer, but what good is it going to do anybody?' And we didn't air it."

"...I don't plan questions. I just get a lot of information about the person I'm interviewing, and when they sit down, I go with what I feel based on their energy, the way they're sitting and a lot of things I just pick up from them. The only time that approach almost backfired was when I was interviewing Michael Jackson. I didn't have any questions prepared, and about five minutes before we went live, I thought, 'What if he doesn't answer?? I'm going to be out of a job.' "

Oprah on Success

"I only came to co-host a talk show because I had failed at news, and I was going to be fired. They tried to convince me at the time that, 'You are so good that you need your own time period, so we are going to give you five minutes at 5:30 in the morning.' I was devastated. I was 22 and embarrassed by the whole thing because I had never failed before. And it was that failure that led to the talk show."

"When I first started being a 'businesswoman,' I worried about, 'How do you do this?' And I realized that you do this the same way as you do anything else. You be fair. You try to be honest with other people, and be fair."

"It doesn't matter who you are, where you come from. The ability to triumph begins with you. Always."

"I decided that I wanted to have more fun in my life, and I've been having a ball. When you make a decision, find the center of your intention, it's amazing how things just turn around."

"The ability to learn to say 'No' and not feel guilty about it is the greatest success I have achieved. For me to have the kind of internal strength and internal courage it takes to say, 'No, I will not let you treat me this way' is what success is all about."

"I don't know if anybody really skyrockets to success. I think that success is a process. I believe that my first Easter speech — at Kosciusko Baptist Church, at the age of 3 1/2 — was the beginning, and that every other speech, every other book I read, every other time I spoke in public, was a building block."

"I think the most important thing to get ahead falls back to what I truly believe in, and that is the ability to seek truth in your life. That's on all forms. You have to be honest with yourself."

"What other people view as successful is not what my idea of success is. What material success does is provide you with the ability to concentrate on other things that really matter. And that is being able to make a difference, not only in your own life, but in other people's lives." ➜

Oprah on the Impact of Books and Reading

"I would have been an entirely different person had I not been taught to read at an early age. My entire life experience, my ability to believe in myself, and even in my darkest moments of sexual abuse and being physically abused and so forth, I knew there was another way. I knew there was a way out. I knew there was another kind of life because I had read about it."

"No one ever told me I was loved. Ever, ever, ever. Reading and being a 'smart girl' was my only sense of value, and it was the only time I felt loved."

"Books opened windows to the world for me. If I can help open them for someone else, I'm happy."

"Knowledge is power. With knowledge, you can soar and reach as high as your dreams will take you."

"When I finished the book, I felt that this was an occasion where the book did more than most books do. Most books tell you a story and let you see what a person's life is like. What 'Beloved' did was let you feel what a person's life was like and feel the exhaustion and devastation of slavery and its impact on one person's life."

PHOTO BY SHOOTING STAR

Oprah on her Personal Life

"I think we (Oprah and Stedman Graham) have a deep love and caring for each other, and respect."

"I think that one of the most important lessons to learn is that we are all responsible for our lives. But nobody gets through this life alone. Everybody needs somebody to show them a way out, or a way up. Everybody does."

"It works so well the way it is, I wouldn't want to mess it up. Which is not to say that we never would get married. But I think that for us, this is what works for now."

"My Aunt Ida chose the name, but nobody really knew how to spell it, so it went down as 'Orpah' on my birth certificate, but people didn't know how to pronounce it, so they put the 'p' before the 'r' in every place else other than the birth certificate. On the birth certificate it is Orpah, but then it got translated to Oprah, so here we are. But that's great because Oprah spells Harpo backwards. I don't know what Orpah spells."

"(My father) can always keep things in perspective for me. I remember my father used to drive me to these speaking contests all over the state. I noticed that the other kids' parents would be jumping up and down when they got third or fourth place, but for my father it was like no big deal."

Quotables

What People are Saying About Oprah

"Oprah set the standard in daytime television. She consistently maintains a decency and morality on her show that gives talk shows a positive name."
— *Rosie O'Donnell*

"I think people like to watch her because she's a master of empathy. Other hosts will say, 'I know how you feel.' But she feels along with you."
— *Sharyn Wolf, a psychotherapist who has appeared on the show as a guest*

"She's a beacon of light; she truly has a mission to empower people. She lives by a mission of grace."
— *Alexandra Stoddard, an interior designer and author who has appeared on the show as a guest*

"Oprah, beautiful, tough and bodacious, is the kind of daughter I would have wanted to have."
— *Maya Angelou, poet*

"I can sum her up in three words: generous in spirit. I was amazed at how available she is to her audience and how interested she is in being of service to them and answering their questions."
— *Actress Kate McGregor-Stewart, after appearing on Oprah's show*

"She's very caring and very committed to helping people,and she gets great satisfaction in seeing people help themselves."
— *Gordon Johnson, President of Hull House*

"If she'd do it, she'd be fantastic. I mean, she's popular, she's brilliant, she's a wonderful woman."
— *Donald Trump, discussing the possibility of running for President with Oprah as his running mate, on "Larry King Live," Oct. 7, 1999*

"I was in shock, I still am. I was used to having my stories published in journals with two copies of it as my payment. (Oprah's) the patron saint of American writers. Thanks to her, I get to have more of a career than I might have."
— *Janet Fitch, author of the novel "White Oleander," on the impact of that book being selected for Oprah's Book Club*

PHOTO BY SHOOTING STAR

Oprah Winfrey